Is 58:12

I have known Tina since college, and she has always had a gift to bridge the gap between people of different races, socioeconomic classes, faiths, and worldviews. She rightly recognizes that all of us long to be reconciled to our Creator and to one another. *Culture Changers* offers a holistic vision for how each of us can be part of that process.

—**REV. DEAN NELSON**, *National Outreach Director for the Human Coalition Action*

For almost twenty years in lay ministry, Tina offered biblical insight to individuals in the areas of spiritual, emotional, and generational healing. She believes that God not only wants to save individual souls but establish godly lineages. Families are the building block of society. In considering how to achieve societal reformation, Tina explains how we must attend to the spiritual, emotional, and physical aspects of our humanity. This book is an excellent resource for those who want to make a difference in their spheres of influence.

—**STEPHEN MCDOWELL**, *President of Providence Foundation, Author of* Monumental—Restoring America as the Land of Liberty Study Guide

In *Culture Changers*, Tina Webb takes bold steps in initiating an honest, faith-based discussion of delicate, race-related subjects. Where others fear to tread, Tina enters headlong. Where others have fallen short, Tina excels in providing a path to true healing for broken individuals.

—**ROB SCHILLING**, *Host and Producer The Schilling Show*

If there has ever been a time in history in which people with wisdom, insight and courage must rise to become culture changers, it is now. Tina not only possesses these very attributes, but she has utilized all of her amazing talent and experience to create this resource to improve ourselves, our families, our communities and our world. This book is a must-read for people desiring to effect positive change in our culture using godly principles.

—CYNTHIA MURRAY, *Divine Women of Destiny Ministries International, Founder/Executive Director, Author and Speaker*

CULTURE CHANGERS

CULTURE CHANGERS

*Understand the Roots of Brokenness and
Help Heal Your Family and Community*

Tina Webb

Carpenter's Son Publishing

Culture Changers: Understand the Roots of Brokenness
and Help Heal Your Family and Community

Copyright ©2020 by Tina Webb

Scripture quotations taken from the New American Standard Bible® (NASB), Copyright © 1960, 1962, 1963, 1968, 1971, 1972, 1973, 1975, 1977, 1995 by The Lockman Foundation. Used by permission. www.Lockman.org

Scripture quotations marked NKJV are taken from the New King James Version of the Bible, copyright ©1982 by Thomas Nelson, Inc. Used by permission.

Scripture quotations marked TPT are from The Passion Translation®. Copyright © 2017, 2018 by Passion & Fire Ministries, Inc. Used by permission. All rights reserved. ThePassionTranslation.com.

Scripture quotations taken from the Amplified® Bible, Copyright © 1954, 1958, 1962, 1964, 1965, 1987 by The Lockman FoundationUsed by permission. (www.Lockman.org)

Cover design by David Stoddard http://mediarevelation.com/
Edited by Lauren Stinton
Interior Layout Design by Suzanne Lawing

ISBN: 978-1-952025-23-5
Printed in the United States of America

For more information visit tinawebb.net

Thank You

I am thankful for my husband and children who encouraged me throughout this process. Thanks to my extended family, friends, and my prayer partners: Eileen, Kelley, Kendra, Tessa, Alayna, Lori, and Sena. This process stretched me, and I needed your prayers! Thank you, Selena, for our talks that helped me flush out many of my thoughts. Thank you, Joan, for women's conferences that launch destiny. Jennifer Miskov, another movement is born! Mom and Julia, thanks for the moments of needed advice. Special thanks to David Stoddard, my patient and encouraging cover designer, and Lauren Stinton, my editor. Also, thanks to Lily and Larry Carpenter for teaching me about the industry. I was new to this process, and you taught me so much. Lastly, thanks to every friend who affirmed my vision to write this book.

Lord, this book belongs to You. You planted the seeds in my heart, watered those seeds through the Writing in the Glory workshop, and guided each step.

Contents

Introduction

Every day we're surrounded by people who are out in the trenches, getting their hands dirty as they change the world. We can see the subtle ripple effects of their efforts—if we're paying attention.

I'm not talking about public servants, although I'm grateful to the millions of nurses, police officers, firefighters, and others who spend their professional lives serving others. My point is that many people, from every background, are working to make a difference in people's lives out of pure compassion.

I've listened to a Caucasian woman who lives in one of the most dangerous inner cities of Mississippi. She shared how she regularly reached out to the African-American drug addict who almost assaulted her. Eventually, he became a family friend. In Cleveland, Ohio lives an African-American leader who grew up in poverty and met a drug dealer while attending college. She ended up pregnant and abused—but she eventually changed the trajectory of her life when someone reached out to her in kindness. Over time she was promoted to lead a division of a national organization that mentors teen moms. I have friends who regularly drive an hour to help a young couple dealing with past trauma find stable footing in their marriage.

All these people—not only are they helping one person find victory, but they're paving the way for entire families to be healthy and the next generation to stand in triumph. They are reforming society one person at a time. I call them Culture Changers.

They're the ones who are going to change the world.

And we can join them.

CHAPTER ONE

Old Situations, New Eyes

People are not disturbed by things,
but by the view they take of them.
EPICTETUS

One humid day in August 2017, the climate of my town shifted. The KKK and Antifa were coming.

Later, some would say that day destroyed the image of Charlottesville and repairing it would take decades. Others said it merely revealed the racism that was already here but ignored. I describe it like this: August 12, 2017, was the beginning of an *unraveling*.

We stayed at home. There was no way we, as an African-American family, were going anywhere near downtown.

That was the plan, anyway, but ironically something came up, and I had to make a quick drive to the downtown area a few hours before the KKK rally was supposed to begin.

I could feel the tension without even getting out of my car, and I prayed as I drove. If I'd been able to see into the spiritual realm, no doubt I would have seen angels on one side with swords in their hands and a demon army on the other, laughing as they invited violence, hate, and murder into my beloved city, where I was raising my children.

There was a murder. A white KKK member ran down a white female protestor with his car. White-on-white crime. Go figure.

I believe that day in 2017 would have been much worse if not for the children of God and their prayers for protection. In advance of the rally, several people gathered at the downtown mall to pray. The storm built threateningly on the horizon, but there they were—followers of Jesus, inviting Him to come and change the situation.

How Brokenness Works

Brokenness permeates our world. It affects all of us, no matter our race, family, or the city or state we were born into. It's a curse passed down through bloodlines. Brokenness builds empires and meets some of us right at our front door. Sometimes literally. I laugh to myself when I recall the house appraiser's face as I answered his knock on our front door. It looked like he didn't expect to see someone who looked like me living here.

My life has given me a unique point of view about race. Although my parents proactively involved us in clubs and events that celebrated our rich African-American heritage, most of my life, I've been immersed in a predominately white world. I homeschooled my children for twenty years—a viable option for many ethnicities. Still, back when I started, it was rare to find a black homeschooling family. For much of my life, my closest friends have been white or Latino, and I've found that what we share bridges our differences. We have many things in common—the desire to be loved, for example. Faith. And brokenness. I've been able to see that white folks have as many issues as black folks. At the same time, I understand the truth of "white privilege," and the white friends I've discussed this with, recognize it as well.

When it comes to emotional needs, we are all the same. All of us face internal struggles, some of them severe, and understanding this one similarity helps us embrace each other. No matter what a person looks like, what club or church they belong to, no matter if they have a college degree or barely made it out of high school—that person is *like us*. Imperfect, but worthy of attention and kindness.

Human brokenness has coursed through history. The issues we face today are not new or "modern" but have been a part of our history since Cain killed Abel. Racism, poverty, and elitism started way before Africans were stolen from their homeland and enslaved. Humanity has been broken—mentally, emotionally, spiritually wounded—for a long time, and this brokenness can show its face in a variety of ways.

Several years ago, a close friend stopped by after work. On the verge of tears, she sat at my kitchen island. She told me about the verbal and emotional abuse she regularly endured from her black co-workers. They called her names, ignored her, and spoke rudely to her. Her attempts to stand up for herself went nowhere.

"They hate me because I'm white," she said, "but I have personally not done anything to them. They don't even know me."

Yes, my friend, I understand. She grew up extremely poor; her parents didn't go to college, and one of her brothers had been in prison. She worked her way through college and cleaned houses after her full-time job each day to help pay her bills. In other words, my white friend understood poverty and struggle, and now she understood the unfairness of being hated based on the color of her skin. For a moment, I felt myself growing angry that those who should know better did this to her.

In another conversation, she and I talked about what it felt like not to belong anywhere. That is, to feel like an outsider. The circle we shared was made up of mostly middle- to upper-class white people with college degrees. Few grew up at her level of poverty or shared my experience as "the only."

As racism cracked open the underbelly of my city and exposed its wounds, August 2017 became seared in mind for another reason. My dad passed away without warning the day after the KKK rally. The whole world seemed to be unraveling right outside my door, and my peace of mind went out the window.

While I believe God was determined to use the evil incidents in my town to unravel the twisted coils of discrimination in the community, He clearly had an agenda for me as well. Surrounded by so much unrest, I grieved and processed death and life, family dysfunction, and community upheaval, as well as the bigger concepts of eternity, the unseen and the visible realms. As the ache in my heart pushed forward, I ended up crying out to God for peace amid so many storms, so many questions, and not enough answers.

I began to think about all I had read over the years— topics like emotional health, cellular memory, spiritual warfare, and quantum physics—and what my husband and I had experienced in our years of ministry. We'd listened to and prayed with many people of various ages, races, and backgrounds. As I considered all these things in the wake of my pain, I began to see the one common denominator—the brokenness spread through society. The course of *inherited sin* rang loud and clear as I recalled how the individuals we ministered to grappled with bad decisions. Decisions they had made on their own, yes, yet they hadn't made them "alone." They were influenced by childhood trauma or family and community culture—more brokenness.

As I pondered these things while watching the news or reading disturbing posts on social media, I prayed again and again, "Lord, I have no idea how You are going to fix this complex mess!"

But at the same time, I had great confidence that He *would* fix it—but it would take more than one U.S. administration, grassroots hashtag, and church prayer meeting. Seeing individual, family, and social struggle through a broader lens and realizing the fixing may take two to three generations has given me a peace that if I do my part, teach my kids to do their parts, and encourage others to do their parts—slowly and steadily, life for us all will improve.

How We View the World

The lens we use to peer into the world around us needs to include how God created humans to function. Not all of the nooks and crannies of our non-physical design can be easily seen and accessed, right there on the surface. Some of them are much more subtle.

For instance, did you know that certain fears and bad habits have generational and spiritual roots? For example, a fear of failure can be passed on and keep each generation from making decisions that benefit them. A lack of preparedness in education can intensify this fear. Similarly, compulsive spending can be an inherited weakness. Twin studies support the genetic components of habits. (We'll talk about this more later in the book.) This issue grows even more complex when we learn those fears and habits can reshape our brains. Multiply this "shaping" times the number of family and community members, and we begin to learn how larger systems—the business world, the political realm, and even faith communities—can become unhealthy and, for some individuals, even destructive.

Here's an everyday example of how this shaping can work. Consider the husband who loses his father to cancer. His grief slowly spirals and pushes him into a depression triggered by his memories of growing up with a dad consumed by work. The adult son realizes he's always longed for quality time with his dad, and now he'll never get it.

His depression causes episodes of anger that begin to affect his wife and kids, as well as the people who work for him. It gets so bad that some employees quit, others become overwhelmed and less productive, and his business begins to suffer.

One man's brokenness not only affects those in his family but reaches out to influence many people in other families, as well as their economies and emotional wellbeing. We aren't islands, and our junk—even the hurts we may not realize exist—can affect others. Our emotional and mental processes influence our behavior and health, and our lives inevitably touch the lives of others. That's how God made us function—as a unit.

A worldview is a lens. When I put on my sunglasses, the lenses influence how I see everything around me. Similarly, how we view the world will dictate how we interpret experiences, issues, and ourselves. When we have a holistic or comprehensive lens, we are empowered. We realize that if we focus on our wellbeing (spirit, soul, and body), and if we strengthen the relationships in our social circles, a domino effect will occur. Just as one person's brokenness can negatively influence the people around him, one person's wellbeing or *triune health*[1] can benefit others.

This route doesn't produce a world without suffering, but it does mean that becoming whole *together* can help us deal with struggles more effectively. When we have a plan for our own triune health and how we're going to help others heal, we become Culture Changers who slowly and steadily mend broken hearts, families, and communities.

The need is all around us. Millions of people long for a nation that offers equality and healing between races, generations, and socioeconomic classes, but much of the climate of present-day America reveals fear and anger instead of hope. From hashtag movements to opioid addiction, statistics and the media reveal people are hurting. This hurt spans political viewpoints and economic class. It is circumstantial (based on individual choices that hurt others), and it is also predictable (because hurting people hurt people).

---

1 Alignment of spirit, soul, and body to the Creator's intent and design.

Embracing the reality of one Creator and understanding the way He designed us to function—as a powerful unit filled with influence—allows us to be equipped to bring wholeness. The world around us can be *changed*—neighborhoods, workplaces, churches. Communities can be transformed one person at a time, one family at a time.

What You Can Expect from This Book

Have you ever looked through a kaleidoscope? As you turn the knob, different layers and designs appear. Going through the material in this book will be a lot like turning the knob of a kaleidoscope back and forth while zooming the picture in and out. I've mentioned some of the problems or symptoms, and later in the book, I'll propose what I consider to be the root and how we can take practical steps to heal it. As we go through this book, we'll understand why the solutions will take time and patience as we walk alongside one another in love.

Remember—change is possible. Hope is coming. Prejudice is *solvable*.

My mother posted this thought on social media a few years ago:

Mostly what we see is "PREJUDICE" — is something we all have. We PRE-JUDGE PEOPLE. We connote things about people that we don't know, from a distance. Prejudice in its highest levels dovetails into racism. But for most of us, prejudging is a part of life and is eradicated when we get to know people individually and see each person's own uniqueness. Prejudice is in our DNA in order to maintain our safety until we know who the person is. It is Stranger Anxiety based on outside appearances. It is understandable. Prejudice can be defeated by conversation and community — by putting on someone else's skin and walking around in it. (Harper Lee – To Kill a Mockingbird.) Prejudice is solvable in communities, in families, and in the individual. Because Love never fails.

The answer is found as we understand one another, and I believe the road is easier to navigate than we think—when paved with commitment and the grace of God.

CHAPTER TWO

Is Something More Serious Going On?

The common eye sees only the outside of things, and judges by that, but the seeing eye pierces through and reads the heart and the soul, finding there capacities which the outside didn't indicate or promise, and which the other kind couldn't detect.
MARK TWAIN

Healing a culture is surprisingly similar to healing a person. As a mom, I know my child is sick when they start displaying visible symptoms like coughing or sneezing. They want to snuggle more than usual, letting me know, "Mommy, I don't feel well." They need me to recognize their pain. Acknowledge their misery. So I have the opportunity to help them emotionally *and* practically. I need to let them know that I feel their pain; that is, when they suffer, I suffer with them. Then I practically ease their discomfort and strengthen their immune system by making them rest and take extra vitamins and supplements. I also pray for them. If the cold doesn't go away after a reasonable period of time, I begin to ask questions. What is keeping their immune system weak? Are they staying hydrated? *Is there something more serious going on?*

Before we look at the process of cultural healing, we must first acknowledge how the symptoms we see or experience make us feel. The issue of racism makes many of us frustrated and angry. Social unrest causes anxiety and criticism. And it's easy to compare ourselves with people that seem to be okay with it all. *They aren't suffering as much as I am.*

In some ways, this could be true. A sick child whose parents can easily buy medicine suffers less than the sick child whose parents have no money even to buy groceries. We can mourn with both, yet acknowledge that one has more stress. When generations of people have been disenfranchised, and the prosperous hear them cry, "we don't feel well," empathy must come before investigating the *why* of the pain. When this is done backward, too often, the problem is focused on, and people's pain is ignored.

But what if their pain makes us uncomfortable? Although some of us seem okay on the outside, shame and embarrassment keep us silent. We feel guilty because we are the parents who can afford the medicine. Accepting our affluence or personal disconnection from affliction doesn't excuse us from acknowledging someone's pain. When one member of a sports team gets injured, the whole team suffers.

All of us deal with the reality that pain is no respecter of persons. We enjoy times of joy and lament times of hardship. But those that are presently sick—those whose symptoms are more apparent—need the less affected members of society to acknowledge their pain.

Although we can hone in on a particular symptom—racial prejudice, for instance, we also have to widen our vantage point. The symptoms vary. But no matter the focus, to bring healing we must acknowledge what others feel; then, we can look at the symptoms and ask questions. *Why* are the symptoms there? Is there something more serious going on? When symptoms persist for generations—as many have, we must find the source of the problem.

When we look at our American society as a whole, we see different symptoms and bigger problems that point toward the need for corporate healing.

Contemporary Symptoms that reflect Historic Roots

No matter who we are—what ethnic make up, we're surrounded by the pain of our history. I learned about the Jewish holocaust and the civil rights movement in my elementary school years. The movies we saw were horrifying: emaciated Jewish women in concentration camps, sullen black men scarred from whips and years of disrespect. I read about Sojourner Truth, whose six-year-old son was mercilessly beaten by his master in Alabama. History affects our present, whether we like it or not, whether we believe such influence is possible or not.

In the past several years, we've seen this influence through protests against racial profiling as well as a renewed outcry for gender equality. Although many colleges created women's studies and other programs two decades ago, unresolved male chauvinism still feeds gender inequality. Scandals in the entertainment industry and the boldness of a fed-up generation birthed the "Me Too" movement that highlights the quietly perpetrated culture of sexual harassment and rape. Systemic inequality is a social and economic reality, and it extends beyond the female fight for equal pay and respect.

As Culture Changers, we benefit when we understand how human brokenness affects the world around us. Gender dynamics and race relations are just two issues. Elitism in economics is another. Some of us believe the chasm between the have and have-nots is maintained by rich people in power who intentionally limit access for those trapped by poverty. Others of us might blame the tension on the poor, citing their neglect of family nurturing, educational opportunities, and financial resources. No matter who we are, what we look like, or what we believe, we are impacted by each other's lens.

Gentrification is a symptom that reveals the overlap of economic subsystems: housing, investing, city planning, etc. Too often, property owners raise the rent on low-income housing so they can force those people out and rebuild for higher income tenants. These property owners and developers are essentially controlling where people live and designing communities to meet not the needs of their current clients, but the desires of clients who can pay them more money. Imagine what it would be like living paycheck to paycheck and barely surviving as a family—and then add to that weight an unsettling fear and bitterness that lower-income people face daily, not knowing if they'll be forced from their homes at any moment.

Discrimination and economics are two major sources of struggle, but for millions of Americans who practice a religion, a changing moral landscape is a symptom of an ailing culture. Even though the United States is home to different belief systems, many of those systems share fundamental views on gender identity, marriage, and abortion. Will they be ridiculed for their beliefs? Will their friends who believe differently than they do walk away from them? Will the holy books of various religions one day be banned because relativism is the new compass for morality?

These issues and so many more can leave us wondering, "What in the *world* will tomorrow bring?" With the advent of a global pandemic, this has become a daily question for all of us.

A Culture Changer resolves to resist the low level of daily anxiety—a quiet, fearful ache that can be hard to ignore. We listen to everyone's concerns. One of our remedies is to "lift up the humble" (Ps. 147:60) and weep with those who weep (Rom. 12:15). Within our hearts is the desire for every individual to have the opportunity to prosper economically, spiritually, and emotionally —holistic healing. Brokenness needs to be addressed in *all areas*, not just the most obvious. People can be broken when they're wealthy, and they can be broken when they're impoverished.

The Root, Not Just the Symptoms

To see tangible results in society, we need to look beyond the pain-ridden *symptoms* to identify the problem's roots. But what does that look like?

When I look at racial discrimination, I can see the root cause is fear. Fear of losing out, fear of losing control, fear of change, etc. From fear comes control and greed. So the question then becomes: How do we get rid of fear? For many of us, that's an easy question—we already know how to answer it because we've been answering it for ourselves or our kids for years. When we're afraid of something, we need to discover the lie that overshadows the truth.

Therefore, the process of healing this pain point in our society looks like speaking into people's fear and helping them to understand what's true, not what is perceived. Once we go through our own seasons of healing in this area, we can then engage different types of people who are struggling *in this same area* and speak comfort to them. Our explanation offers them a clearer lens, "We don't need to be afraid here because this person or these people are like us. Let's not allow the *externals* to dictate truth, but acknowledge the essence of their humanity. We will make ourselves stronger by claiming them instead of rejecting them."

If you're familiar with the biblical story of the Good Samaritan, you recognize that God has a way of turning a nation's story upside down. The hated guy—the Samaritan, whose people were oppressed—went out of his way to take care of one of his oppressors. He didn't react in fear or hatred but stooped down to show compassion—what a statement. And what a quiet announcement to his fellow Samaritans: "If we want to change the situation, we need to love the very people who are perpetrating the situation."

We can change culture by the way we live and how we treat those who hate us.

Brokenness Knows No Color

As we've come to understand, we're all *broken*. The symptoms of our dilemma show themselves on our bad days—when we are tired, overwhelmed, and hampered by personal struggle.

Hurting people don't live just in inner cities, nor are they simply those who suffer from depression or physical issues—they're your next-door neighbor and college roommate, your boss, and your mother. Whether your neighbor is the wealthy wife of a lawyer who never experienced an emotional connection with her mother, or the athlete in your son's high school whose recent injury just ended his collegiate prospects, hurting people exist everywhere. No one is exempt from emotional pain.

Despite the layered symptoms that we see every day, we can position ourselves to find the cure—the solution that will help heal our culture.

Dreams allow us to strive for a better future, no matter how impossible it seems. This work is day to day, little by little, and if we want to see immediate results, we will be disappointed. If we allow ourselves to be overwhelmed by the symptoms—the giants that we see every day—we will remain stagnant. Healing takes time. The poet Langston Hughes wrote that daily life can be a dream killer.

> Bring me all your dreams,
> You dreamer,
> Bring me all your
> Heart melodies
> That I may wrap them
> In a blue-cloud cloth
> Away from the too rough fingers
> Of the world.[1]

Here's one of my dreams. When I think of "valleys being exalted," as Isaiah 40:4 talks about, I envision decaying rural and urban areas and their residents given the value they deserve and the attention they need. I see private, home, and public high school students doing service projects to fix shutters and pull weeds. I see mom groups taking groceries and recipes to new moms, whether they live in the inner city or the suburbs. I see male pastors walking down streets, some with manicured lawns and some littered by garbage, asking for names and giving a father-hug to the fatherless.

The best way to see the people around us overcome personal and family dysfunction, the trauma of discrimination, and systemic corruption might surprise you because it's so simple.

Hard, yes. Time-consuming, yes.

But the answer to many of the big questions we're asking today is one-on-one relationship.

NOTES
1. Langston Hughes, *The Dream Keeper and Other Poems* (New York: Alfred A. Knopf, 1986), 3

CHAPTER THREE

How You Can Start Thinking Like a Culture Changer

I've learned to pay attention to my words—casual statements that I make. Why? Because *how we say* what we say can reveal fears or pain that we carry from the past. Is there often cynicism or sarcasm in our tone? When a person shares an opposing political viewpoint, are we condemning or quick to dismiss? Do we counter their opinion before considering its merit? The fears and wounds we carry will creep into our conversations if not resolved. Recognizing our pain, and then obtaining closure, helps us no longer react. Healing removes the pressure points of past trauma.

Despite our shortcomings and the things we still struggle with, human beings—each of us has a beautiful gift to give the world. The darker the night, the brighter the star. Aristotle said, "It is during our darkest moment that we must focus to see the light." That darkest hour causes us to look around for any flicker of light.

Many of us sang "This Little Light of Mine" when we were kids. We belted out the words with enthusiasm and intent. Children somehow know the light of God—vitality, soundness of mind, peace, beauty, goodness, understanding—can repel the world's darkness. Enamored with divine purpose, we were ready to go out and conquer the darkness threatening the land. Heroes and heroines of real-life fairytales.

But then something happened. Many of us walked head-first into hurtful experiences that traumatized us. We ended up adopting attitudes and behaviors we saw in older family members, and these things worked to pull blinders over our eyes. Our enthusiasm for destroying darkness gradually morphed into apathy and skepticism—our whole-hearted passion became stunted.

Heaven on Earth

If you're like me, you're an optimist who has overcome hurdles and see that the mountain top of your life is closer than the valley you left behind. You recognize and sometimes experience injustice, but you try not to let it get under your skin because you genuinely believe things can change. You want the ideal for everyone, no matter what ethnicity, nationality, or generation—or in other words, you're after heaven on earth.

When I realized I would never be perfect this side of heaven, it was a massive blow to my ego. The reality of my brokenness washed me with shame, and I began to struggle with self-condemnation and a general sense of being a failure. This realization also made me critical of others. By magnifying other people's faults as well as my own, I didn't feel so bad about myself.

But gradually, God began to teach me about grace and mercy, process, and maturity. As I began to heal, I learned to extend this newfound understanding to others, even those who had hurt me. I realized that each of us carries buried pain and gets triggered by each other's issues and current events—and our bag of stress gets spilled out on people around us. If I was not going to be perfect in this lifetime, then neither will anyone else. We are all works in progress.

As Culture Changers, we are visionaries and trouble-shooters. No one's potential should be wasted, so we want to get out there and dirty our hands with the hard work of turning systemic failures into life-giving processes. Death to life—that is a foundational thought for every Culture Changer. Yet we're still learning what this looks like practically and how to carry it out in everyday situations.

The realization that all of us—man, woman, and child, were born into an imperfect world doesn't excuse abuse, misuse, and injustice. But it does give us a broader view of the human condition, which partners with understanding what God is after. People can change when given the right tools.

From Broken to Whole

Brokenness is the tendency toward destructive rather than constructive movement. This tendency is often passed down from generation to generation and permeates every aspect of life. Every family is affected, and since people build systems, brokenness also infiltrates the manmade systems all around us.

Wholeness is perfect alignment between every aspect of our immaterial (spirit and soul) and physical (body) composition. When our triune composition is out of joint with God's design, life doesn't flow the way it should. We become hindered spiritually, emotionally, and biologically. Picture someone's elbow out of joint. The nerves and blood are constricted and unable to move freely according to their normal, unhindered paths. But once the bone is put back into place, everything works the way it is supposed to.

When wholeness or alignment happens in our lives, *shalom* can flow unhindered. The Hebrew word *shalom* is a state of peace, completeness, harmony, and security. From this state, we reflect the goodness of our Creator to everyone and everything around us. The blinders begin to fall away; mindsets shift, and divine purpose breaks forth.

We were made for shalom—an individual ideal with corporate benefits. Humanity is like a building constructed of stones, one set securely on top of another. *Loose* stones clearly affect the whole structure. As hearts are healed and thinking transformed, we as a society become steady where we used to be shaky. Our health builds up the entire structure instead of being a liability.

As we become more and more *whole*, not only do we experience vitality as individuals, but our vitality blossoms outward to affect everyone around us. The building becomes more stable.

Some belief systems teach the idea of *enlightenment* or self-realization. This is the idea of finding ultimate goodness and knowledge, or a state of perfection, in one's self. The difference between enlightenment and the Hebrew idea of shalom is the object worshiped. Enlightenment believes that humanity within itself has the capacity for "godhood," while the heart of shalom worships God as the Creator of everything, as stated in Colossians 1. The Bible teaches that our "best" doesn't come in this earthly life, but to the degree we experience shalom in every part of our beings—body, soul, and spirit—the more effectual and life-giving our time on earth will be.

Looking Up, Looking In, Looking Out

Every great dream begins with a dreamer. Always remember, you have within you the strength, the patience, and the passion to reach for the stars to change the world.
HARRIET TUBMAN

As we become whole as individuals, our families and communities get to experience the benefits. This gradually leads to legacies of healthy emotional connection, wise stewardship, and economic innovation. Communities like mine in Charlottesville, Virginia, can become genuinely unified—as individuals are healed.

That is the life-giving mission motivating every Culture Changer. We can remember when we were depressed or addicted, the times we felt unwanted and disrespected; we remember all those years of battling hopelessness. Despite our good intentions, many of us have mindsets, habits, and manners still in need of *unraveling*, so we can develop a more natural bent toward mercy—honoring people for who they are and not what they have done.

We've experienced a degree of victory over many challenges. Our lives have changed, and we feel an urge to wade back out on to the battleground and help our brothers and sisters who are still struggling. We have come to own our sto-

ries—incredible testimonies, all of them—and now can partner them with a holistic, full-picture understanding, which
enables us to come alongside anyone and do the work of a
Culture Changer. "What do you need? I can help you."

> So then, strengthen hands that are weak and knees that
> tremble. Cut through and make smooth, straight paths
> for your feet [that are safe and go in the right direction],
> so that the leg which is lame may not be put out of joint,
> but rather healed. (Heb. 12:12–13 AMP)

Some people will not be ready for change—that is a universal reality. They may be afraid of losing what is familiar to
them. Change can be uncomfortable. If someone is not ready
to make the necessary adjustments that will benefit them, we
must respect that. But it doesn't change who we are and what
we're called to do. We are called to extend our hand.

Think of Sean, the therapist in the movie *Good Will
Hunting*. He didn't force Will to change, but he waited until
the younger man was ready to deal with his inner turmoil.[2]
That is our model of loving someone in the midst of their
brokenness. We love well and wait when we need to, giving
people time.

Healing: A Chain Reaction

A Culture Changer is a reformer, a term that's commonly
used in reference to the Protestant Reformation of the six-
teenth century. *The Cambridge English Dictionary* defines the
word *reform* as a person who works for political, social, or
religious change. We might call a reformer a *systemic trouble-
shooter*, someone who sees problems and directs their efforts
toward finding improvement. This is similar to the idea of

activism, but activism also includes the desire and action to *impede* anything that opposes a person or group's worldview or the efforts to advance the reform they feel is necessary. Activism can be positive or negative, depending on which side you're on, but I consider *reformation* or this *remaking* to be a consistently positive approach to change. Again and again, I have seen people embrace personal reformation and start to leave healing and wholeness everywhere they go.

When someone decides to change their direction, they move from brokenness toward triune health. Their life begins to step into the shalom of God, and people around them benefit. Here are a few examples of what this can look like:

- A workaholic, driven by performance addiction because of his lack of affirmation as a child will now be emotionally and physically present for his children, able to impart a sense of importance and security to another generation. Personal reformation will dramatically affect his children's future productivity in society.

- The surgeon who once struggled with self-centeredness and elitism becomes free not only to mentor doctors and fellow surgeons but also to encourage them to step out of their comfort zones—to go to economically disadvantaged areas around the world to perform surgeries and give aid to those in desperate need.

- Franchise owners who have realized their ability to help and restore others will build stores in poor communities and provide their local residents access to training, jobs, and mentoring. People of different economic backgrounds will have the opportunity to interact and learn from one another.

- Veteran teachers or administrators can start support groups for teachers who feel burned out. They will refresh their vision, listen to their concerns, and give them creative ideas. A teacher's enthusiasm transfers to the students and the school staff, which in turn has a huge impact on the local community.

- The young man who is struggling to keep a job because of his addictions and lack of self-discipline will meet a Culture Changer who can relate to him and offer him what he needs: short-term goals that will give him a sense of accomplishment, as well as tough love and accountability as he defeats his "inner demons."

- The cleaning company owner will desire to mentor others in small business entrepreneurship. His new paradigm of selflessness and inventiveness leads him to find school custodial workers who need extra money and can be paid as private contractors, thus increasing their economic status. He can mentor them on how to create their own small cleaning enterprise, which promotes dignity and self-confidence—two things that have the power to impact a person dramatically.

- Employers and employees, CEOs, pastors, the police officers—these people in key positions in a city will have the emotional and spiritual health that fosters goodwill, innovation, and notable character.

Do you see what *you* could do—the immense impact you could have—simply by getting healthy and then choosing to come to the aid of someone in need? Culture Changers benefit society at a foundational level, and the benefit never actually stops because it spreads from person to person, layer upon layer.

NOTES
2. Miramax Films presents a Lawrence Bender production; a film by Gus Van Sant; produced by Lawrence Bender; written by Matt Damon & Ben Affleck; directed by Gus Van Sant. Good Will Hunting. [Santa Monica, Calif.]: Lionsgate, 2011. P.22

CHAPTER FOUR

A Knee-Jerk Culture

I shall allow no man to belittle my soul
by making me hate him.
BOOKER T. WASHINGTON

I resisted social media for years and only began using it as my siblings had children and friends moved away. It became a way to stay in touch.

But these days I don't log in much anymore, and maybe you can guess why. One of the unfortunate byproducts of social media is that it offers the ease of quick engagement for users. But hurting people hurt people. Broken people break people. Turmoil takes center stage in social media again and again. Every day we find ourselves with multiple opportunities to react to other people's viewpoints. Pick any even remotely controversial post, glance through the comments, and you'll inevitably find a fiery dialogue between those of opposing views. Mutual respect has been replaced by quick reactions, vehement rejections, and condemning putdowns— all of which are demonstrations of how hostility has become socially acceptable in our culture. Consequently, social media has become a turn-off for many people.

But honestly, the blame can't fall only on the platform of social media. Many people simply don't agree to disagree.

The Beauty of an Unoffendable Heart

Without really thinking about it, many people assume the word *different* somehow means unrelatable or even unlike-able, but that is not true. That definition is the staple of partisan politics. But what is *different* can be beneficial. Differing perspectives occur all the time between husbands and wives, although each sees the same situation. To solve a family problem together, they need the other person's point of view. As far as the word *different* meaning unfamiliar or unrelatable, this is a common perception. All of us are comfortable with what we know—the familiar. In middle school, I noticed that even though my friends and I had been together in elementary school, we started to sit only with kids of the same race. Gravitating to people who look like us is not unhealthy—*preferring people who look like us is*. We can learn how to shrug off discomfort and fear to reach out and embrace people of different backgrounds. To bring healing to our communities, we all must do this.

When I was young, my family and I lived in a diverse community of Jewish people, Catholics, and Protestants. Some of us were white, and some of us were black. As kids, we acknowledged our differences but weren't insulted by them. I learned that my fourth-grade buddy's family ate matzah and didn't believe Jesus was God. Jonathan's mom let me try matzah one day, and I think she could tell by the look on my face that I didn't like it! I thought my dislike might offend her, but she just smiled.

Months later, Jonathan invited me to his birthday party at the Jewish Community Center, and I was the only black person there. Despite feeling a little overwhelmed by the cultural differences, I knew Jonathan and his family liked me, which made everything alright.

My few Catholic friends also had some different beliefs than I did. I went to a mass once and decided at eleven that I liked my faith expression better. The friend who invited me wasn't offended. It was normal to respect differences of opinion; it was okay for each of us to think "our" way was the best. Jewish, Catholic, or Protestant, when we were in each other's houses, we knew to respect "house rules" even if we didn't participate or personally agree with them. We never became offended and thought the "house rules" were discriminatory—I never expected Jonathan's mom to serve me pork just because I liked pork. It was our choice to go to that friend's house or not.

Somehow as a culture, we've lost the ability to respect different beliefs and points of view. So often, if someone hears a view that is different than their own, they lash out. The offended demands the other to rethink their stance.

I believe this inability for people to engage civilly with others is a sign of how much fear reigns in our culture right now. Each of us *fears* that an opposing position will become the "norm" in our culture, which will then turn our nation into something we despise. The consequence of this fear is that a contrary view is shut down by the power of the loudest voice.

We must conform to a popular narrative, and if we do not, we are shunned. Unfortunately, the fear of being ostracized for one's beliefs keeps many silent and emboldens others.

Be Careful What You Say and How You Say It

Hidden within our culture is a trend toward a hypersensitivity. To be accepted and not offend, a new set of language rules was born, commonly referred to as "political correctness." The problem with political correctness is that it is rooted in fear and control, and no one can build a healthy society when fear and control are the foundation.

Political correctness began as an attempt to erase the possibility of offense for the historically marginalized. A good idea in theory, yet the heightened sensitivity it has produced in our nation has stimulated a *reaction culture*. Political correctness has taught us to pay attention to slights and belief systems, and as a nation, we've become afraid to share our views. *How will they react if they find out what I believe?* We are afraid that someone will be offended.

Some traditional ideas are obviously no longer appropriate. For instance, not every doctor is male, nor is every nurse female. Not everyone who delivers your mail is a "mailman." It is appropriate that some wording and certain barriers have been crossed in our culture.

However, somewhere along the way, spiritual beliefs and some moral views have gotten swept up in the stream of *politically inappropriate*. The idea of marriage being between only one man and one woman is an example. Today that belief offends many people—you could even lose your job and be publically renounced if you declare what you believe in this regard. Yet many faiths—Muslim, Hindi, Sikh, Jewish, and

Christian—hold to this traditional view of marriage. Similarly, belief in God is mocked in many secular institutions, which puts millions of people of various faiths on the defensive. When it comes to religious and socio-political issues like gender identity and the unborn, pronouns like *he, she,* and words like *preborn*, have been replaced by terms that don't "offend."

Certain beliefs are no longer welcome in the educational sector and are ignored by the media pulpit. When we stay silent because we're afraid of offending the insatiable appetite of political correctness, we invite *the loudest voice* to dictate what is morally and ethically acceptable. Voices ignored are voices unheard. Unfortunately, that is a byproduct of political correctness.

When we look at society with open eyes and a sensitive heart, we can see that political correctness cannot solve the problem of fear in people's hearts. At the end of the day, it doesn't bring the comfort we were hoping for—it brings control and silence.

Who is Triggered?

Rioting is a childish way of trying to be a man, but it takes time to rise out of the hell of hatred and frustration and accept that to be a man you don't have to riot.
ABRAHAM MASLOW, AN AMERICAN PSYCHOLOGIST

As I shared earlier, my city of Charlottesville found itself the center of national attention when the KKK decided to hold a rally in the downtown area to protest the removal of a Confederate statue. Anarchists and activists poured into my small college town. Proponents and opponents of the statue's demise showed up as well. They had all been triggered. A trigger is an unconscious psychological mechanism that prompts a reaction. Attendees were motivated by their anger, reasonable concerns, or a desire to promote social unrest.

I believe triggers are a reason for some police shootings of black males. I have four sons, and these incidents alarm me. I often pray for divine protection for my adult sons when they leave the house. Many of these incidents are conscious and intentional, but some are not—they are an outcome of the subconscious trigger of fear. A trigger is often based on a stereotype.

I know a woman I will call Susan who was in a relationship with someone of another race. After being emotionally and physically abused, Susan ended the relationship, but for a time she was triggered whenever she saw someone of the same build and skin color. We all do it, often without realizing it. We can be *triggered* by something that reminds us of painful episodes in our personal history.

As I've worked toward my own emotional healing and practiced becoming more self-aware, I'll often notice a sudden sensitivity to one of my kids or my husband. I try to pause *before* I respond to them and ask myself, "Why am I triggered?" Those of us who are married or have kids benefit when we recognize our triggers and take some time to figure out their origin. The more I deal with these origins, the less I operate in projection, reaction, and conflict.

All of us are linked—by geography, history, traditions, as well as significant events like 9/11 and the COVID-19 pandemic. Because of our link, triggers aren't just personal; they can also be corporate. This corporate trigger is based on a shared experience. Like war. Or discrimination. Or persecution. As Culture Changers, we have to look at the cause for personal and corporate triggers and deal with them correctly.

Demonizing One, Giving a Pass to Another

As we readjust our lenses to find ways to heal the *whole* person, we have to remember that there are wounded people everywhere. Some wear the mask of "I'm good!" But many people are barely surviving emotionally. They might be your neighbor. Or your doctor. Or a political leader.

The "court of public opinion" needs to evaluate all moral offenses equally and not just acknowledge those that are the "hot spots" of media focus. We cannot demonize the athlete who endorses the candidate we view as immoral and turn the other cheek for the entertainer whose videos feature women as props and toys. We can't punish one person and give the other, or ourselves, a free pass. Because all humanity is broken, those in positions of influence cannot be expected to be perfect and infallible. While their actions and words need to be reviewed and consequences dispensed if they break the law, as Culture Changers, our motivation is assisting any person, regardless of their position, on the path toward wholeness. The Book of Ecclesiastes reminds us that the emotional needs of the oppressor should not be ignored. Impartiality recognizes the flawed humanity in all of us.

Culture Changers come to the aid of any person, from the well-known individual to the homeless man whose name has been forgotten, in order to show love and help guide that person out of dark times. In every case, you and I can view these individuals as broken, humbly pray for them, and applaud them when they overcome. A traditional Protestant hymn says, "There is none righteous, no not one." Instead of pointing out one another's faults, we can turn and offer a helping hand—one that patiently encourages hope and healing.

> *If one by one we counted people out*
> *For the least sin, it wouldn't take us long*
> *To get so we had no one left to live with.*
> *For to be social is to be forgiving.*
> ROBERT FROST

CHAPTER FIVE

Victimhood and Our Response

We wear the mask that grins and lies,
It hides our cheeks and shades our eyes,—
This debt we pay to human guile;
With torn and bleeding hearts, we smile.
PAUL LAURENCE DUNBAR

"With torn and bleeding hearts, we smile."

What a true statement. Maybe we don't wear a mask, and we'd never consider ourselves a victim, but I believe many of us still put on a mask—to hide who we are, to present instead something we think others want. I think of "human guile" as *craftiness*. Remember when you were a kid, and you tried not to get caught doing something sneaky? Or maybe you had to think quickly to piece together a reasonable account of what you and your friends were doing after school, hiding what actually happened.

For those of us who are well acquainted with our crafty or wounded pasts, we smile and chuckle about our youthful escapades. We smile while we pretend, yet the smile doesn't erase the real pain inside—the shame. No cover can take that away. We hide being a victim of our former misdeeds and inevitably fall victim to the mask.

Maybe you were a good kid and never got into trouble. Perhaps you grew up in a safe and loving environment. But as I'm sure you've experienced, a safe and loving home life doesn't guarantee an absence of pain. Maybe one of your parents faced failure, and it pulled the rug out from under your sense of security. Sometimes the wound that hurts us isn't our own—someone else's wound will bleed on us. Eventually, we all become a victim of something.

When I was in fifth grade, I became a victim of other people's opinions. One day, a black classmate called me an "Oreo." I didn't know what that meant, but I knew it was mean. Another friend explained, "cause you talk white." To them, I was black on the outside but white on the inside. Their put-down made me angry because I couldn't help that my parents and grandparents made me pronounce each word clearly. This experience led to a fear of being rejected and produced other insecurities within me. I had become a victim of someone else's broken mindset. Verbal, emotional, and physical trauma destroy our God-given dignity and sense of worth. Even trauma as minor as what I experienced in fifth grade can cause pain that lasts for years, and it isn't always pain that other people can see.

One of the consequences of being a victim is developing an unhealthy "victim mentality" or *identity* that must be discarded as we are made whole. If we grew up in poverty, a subconscious fear of lack can remain even when we've left poverty behind. This fear will show itself in our decisions and behaviors. In addition, we can carry emotional pain from our forefathers in our DNA, and this pain—though it "began" potentially hundreds of years ago—can affect us to the point of influencing our outlook on life.

A victim mentality can even cause people to exert their fear and resentment through violence. Stored-up emotion finds a release at some point. All of us have probably heard stories of rioters and vandals taking advantage of storms, power outages, and public unrest in New York City; Ferguson, Missouri; and many other cities. It doesn't matter whether or not the store is owned by a person who looks just like the rioter—resentment and pain are color-blind.

The Problem of Poverty

If the misery of the poor be caused not by the laws of nature, but by our institutions, great is our sin.
CHARLES DARWIN

Many religious texts talk about the disparities between the rich and the poor. A general summary of Hindu belief is that a person must accept whatever life they were born into and not look for its condition to change because the next life may be different.

The Buddhist stance is different. It views poverty as a result of governmental and public apathy toward the needy.

However, in Buddhism, the lack of material goods is noble because acquiring "things" produces internal distress. In other words, when you don't have much, you have less to worry about.

Judaism and Christianity offer an even different approach to understanding and dealing with poverty. Psalm 9 shares various verses that express empathy and guidance so people can actually *escape* the condition of poverty:

> *And those who know Your name will*
> *put their trust in You (v. 10).*
>
> *God does not forget the cry of the afflicted (v. 12).*
>
> *For the needy will not always be forgotten nor the hope*
> *of the afflicted perish forever (v. 18).*

Judaism and Christianity offer a way *out* of poverty, as well as justice for those who have been trapped by it. Poverty is viewed as a curse—a destructive consequence of original sin. Part of the remedy is the *release* from the curse. How? First, by trusting in God, the Creator, who does not ignore those who come to Him in their time of need. The writer of Psalms continues with a warning to civic, federal, and other organized systems and structures. There will be a harsh consequence for all people and systems that have made "nets" to trap people:

> *The nations have sunk down in the pit which they made;*
> *In the net which they hid, their own foot is caught.*
> *The* Lord *is known by the judgment He executes;*
> *The wicked is snared in the work of his own hands. (vv. 15–16)*

A net is a manmade tool that inhibits movement, life, and freedom. So according to this verse, the oppressors will themselves be caught, and the civic, federal, and other organized systems will be trapped in their own corruption.

Can injustice be corrected? Isaiah 59:8 offers a unique answer that differs from other religions as it describes "crooked paths." Christianity views poverty and inequality as products of a path that is crooked, while God desires a straight road. C. S. Lewis wrote, "A man does not call a line crooked unless he has some idea of a straight line."[3] Dr. Martin Luther King challenged Americans to admit that the way to a thriving America cannot involve the factor of inequality. Poverty is not to be accepted nor viewed as noble. Crooked paths must be made straight.

> *The way of peace they have not known,*
> *And there is no justice in their ways;*
> *They have made themselves crooked paths;*
> *Whoever takes that way shall not know peace.*
> ISAIAH 59:8

People control systems, and while many individuals will one day be indicted for their misdeeds, our goal as Culture Changers is not the punishment of a crime—but the transformation of a soul. The unhealthy mindsets and the unhealed issues of the heart cause people to be corrupt and take advantage of the needy. So another way to be released from the curse is to change the hearts of those that maintain systems of poverty. God wants to rescue *all* parties involved, not just the victim.

Who Will Comfort the Oppressor?

One of the "difficult points" in this topic of wholeness is the idea of extending compassion or mercy to an oppressor—someone who has injured others and continues to rule over them.

But if no one takes this risk, it is likely the oppressor's heart will not be changed, which means systemic oppression will not be changed either. When a leader stays corrupt, the people continue to suffer. So someone needs to be brave and choose to help the leader.

Compassion feels sorrow and empathy; it acknowledges the pain others feel. It weeps with those who weep. Some are victims—not because their ancestors were brutalized, but because their ancestors were brutal. These individuals are victims of their bloodline. They've inherited more than wealth, position, and influence; blindness and denial fill their souls. These descendants of slave owners and overseers carry their own kind of grief. They bear "scarlet letters" and have to deal with the aftermath of the trading and enslavement of their fellow man. Corporate healing means that *every* soul can process the dark realities of its family lines.

As I stated before, the pain of some makes others uncomfortable. Shame stifles the humanity of the "uncomfortable," causing them to brush over the hard-to-read news articles that highlight another person's turmoil. Many people like this want the country to "move on" from issues like racism, yet this attitude doesn't help those who actually can't move on because their lives are still trapped by racism.

It is human to feel sorrow for the wickedness our ancestors perpetrated; it is human to feel emotional at the pain others have endured as a result of our ancestors' mentalities and actions. This shame and guilt will remain intact—*until* they are relinquished into the faithful hands of a gracious Redeemer. God doesn't want *anyone* to live in guilt or shame. Ecclesiastes confirms this sentiment. "Then I looked again at all the acts of oppression which were being done under the sun. And behold I saw the tears of the oppressed and that they had no one to comfort them; and on the side of their oppressors was power, but *they* had no one to comfort them.[2]

White guilt is a merciless oppressor. And it is irrational—no one chooses their skin color. While white people can certainly help to undo the active consequences of their ancestors' sin, they should not accept blame *for* their sin, loathe the color of their skin, or take responsibility for unseen forces that continue to drive systemic racism.

History has caused us to consider the oppressor too often through the lens of race. I believe one reason we're seeing an increasing number of young white males joining hate groups is that the brokenness in our society has told them their skin color makes them "oppressors." It doesn't matter if they grew up poor, without opportunity, and in need of as much public assistance as their counterparts in another racial group—they're still oppressors because of their skin color. Making generalizations—one ethnic group as the only victims and another as the oppressors is dangerous because it fuels bitterness and increases division.

When we look back through time, we do see European dominance through colonization. But if we separate the various ethnicities within Europe, we find both oppressors and

---

2 Ecclesiastes 4:1

the oppressed. We can also find similar situations within non-white people groups. Asian, Middle Eastern, and African history have evidence of one tribe or clan being a victim of another. Furthermore, is it biblical to consider the oppressor solely on the scale of their control? For example, a man who beats his wife is an oppressor. Gangs of every race oppress some neighborhoods. Middle Eastern girls are forced to marry adult men; their childhood is stolen before puberty. Demons oppress all of us at times. Unfortunately, when we focus on our human enemies, the real enemy stays hidden. We tend to focus on our personal experience with victimhood so much that we often don't think about the narrative we find ourselves in—an on-going story of good versus evil. We are part of a more significant dilemma.

In chapter 7, we'll talk about the origin of sin and evil, but the Bible teaches there is a spiritual entity behind the evil we see around us. He doesn't care what skin-color a person is; he victimizes everyone. So the real war is "not with flesh and blood."[3] Our unseen enemy stifles triune healing to keep us a victim of our pain. Moreover, this enemy seeks to steal, kill, and destroy our humanity, and one subtle way he does this is by getting us to fight each other, by suppressing our compassion for one another and through unforgiveness.

Our desire for justice is legitimate, but what can we do when the justice system is broken? As a woman and a person of slave descent, what brings me peace is the promise of God to individually and corporately rescue. For the poor, needy,

---

3 Ephesians 6:12

and oppressed, the Judeo-Christian God offers encouragement that the poor and oppressed will be remembered and saved. The practical questions are *when* and *how*.

The other day I listened to a sermon where the pastor led the congregation in a time of prayer. He started praying for victims—but then he took a turn I didn't expect. He prayed for the *victimizers* who were in the church. He prayed something like this: "You may have been molested, or you may be the molester. It was your fault, and you carry the shame of messing up someone else's life. God wants to heal you too."

Mic drop! That is taking forgiveness and brokenness to a whole new level. It is putting into practice the reality that even the *oppressor* is a victim. The pastor's prayer of healing didn't erase the consequences the victimizer faced, but it extended grace and the power to change his heart. In this situation, the scripture that I quoted before—"As a man thinks in his heart, so is he"—can be put into practice in a supernatural way. Now the victimizer can think of himself as forgiven, clean, and pure, and he will begin a process of learning how to operate out of that identity.

Have you ever wondered how the parent or spouse of a murder victim can go to the killer after court and forgive them? I sure have. I'm sure the parent or spouse is still in pain—but they have determined *not* to be a victim of the other person's crime by carrying unforgiveness in their heart.

Me Versus the Other

Both my mother and my husband were sociology majors. I never had an interest, but after reviewing the dynamics of society, family background, and human relationships, I've been fascinated by the subject. Unpacking a few sociological ideas is helpful if we are to help ourselves and others begin to heal.

Victimization will always exist where there is ego. The root of ego is self. From this primary identity comes the ability to be selfish, self-serving, and "me" centered. Sociologists such as George Herbert Mead have written books about the theory of "self" as it relates to the concept of "other." Both our social experience and our families indirectly teach us how to relate to others and be viewed by others.

Children cannot embrace autonomy the way adults do. Their identity is tied to belonging to a defined family system whose views are naturally passed down. While some of this is critical for healthy human development, at some point, we have to stop and evaluate what we "caught" from our family systems and what was explicitly taught by our family members. What did we pick up that affects our views of others? For example, some children are taught that their ethnic group is smarter than other ethnic groups. Others are told that all homeless people are drunks or that people are poor only because they are lazy. To embrace our individuality as kids, we learned to contrast ourselves with others through the process of comparison.

Are All Humans Equal?

Comparison is inevitable as we define ourselves and learn about the world around us. I was a Northerner for the first eighteen years of my life, and during that time, I "learned" that Southern people were not as smart because they weren't as articulate. They were friendly—but not as smart, while Northerners were smart but not as friendly. I have no idea where I picked up those beliefs. We all "catch" and keep unfortunate stereotypes that can subtly or directly push us toward deepening one another's wounds.

As children develop a sense of self, they inevitably become aware of differences. This awareness is healthy; problems begin only when physical or social distinctions are viewed antagonistically. We need to teach children to view differences under the light of a shared human canvas. Our shared humanity should be celebrated, our divinely ordained distinctions appreciated. As Culture Changers, our goal is to dismantle divisive *manmade* distinctions.

> *In recognizing the humanity of our fellow beings, we pay ourselves the highest tribute.*
> THURGOOD MARSHALL

> *There is neither Jew nor Greek, there is neither slave nor free man, there is neither male nor female; for you are all one in Christ Jesus.*
> GALATIANS 3:28

In Galatians 3:28, we find a simple revelation of God's perspective of humanity. While the context is for those who subscribe to the Christian faith, the verse communicates God's intent that we see each other outside of the lenses we commonly use. No matter our ethnicity, social position, or biological gender, we are all made in the image of God. Because not every person or religion agrees with this biblical perspective, sometimes, the issue of human rights comes into play.

Consider the Chinese practice of preferring male babies to female babies, the Muslim practice of elevating males above women and children, the Hindu caste system, and the global problem of enslaving adults and children. Various cultures measure people based on their biology, economic status, educational achievement, or how someone can profit them.

Think about your opinion on human equality. In your view, should we stand up for the equal rights of women in other countries or stand back to respect cultural preferences? Which position is moral?

Generally speaking, the idea of worth in our culture is based not only on economic or social status but also on the quality of life and a person's age. Some use those factors to judge another person's value. We can find ready examples of this mindset on the news as they report on endorsing euthanasia of the sick and elderly or abortion for babies with Down's syndrome. Throughout history and in every nation, men have exerted dominance over other men through tribal warfare, colonialism, and class systems. News of horrific evils like mass shootings, genocide, trafficking, and other forms of forced labor are in the news daily. These people are victims of manmade distinctions. When we consider Galatians 3:28 as the best lens through which to view humanity, the problem becomes apparent—some people just don't believe we were all created equal. They rebel against the idea; they resent it and undermine its reality. At the heart of certain issues exists a lust for domination that threatens the health of society. According to the words of Thurgood Marshall, former Supreme Court Justice, we do not "pay ourselves the highest tribute" when we mistreat our fellows.

The way we view and treat others shows our morality. In a society where viewpoints are wide-ranging and often culturally based, the idea of fairness and the fight for rights becomes problematic. In the United States, guaranteeing equal rights often becomes a part of legislation and political conversations, but because many citizens base their moral views on culture or faith, it is difficult to enact laws that do not step on someone's toes.

Jesus Christ teaches a powerful lesson on societal relationships in Mark 12:31, where He said simply, "You shall love your neighbor as you love yourself." The context of this Scripture is that our "neighbor" is the person in need. His statement implies two points: first, to the degree that we love, care for, and honor ourselves, we can do the same for those in need; second, our ability or inability to receive God's love is reflected in how we treat others. In other words, we cannot love well if we do not understand how much the Creator loves us. We cannot show mercy if we cannot receive mercy.

In another passage of the New Testament, Jesus discusses loving our enemies:

> *But I say to you, love your enemies, bless those who curse you, do good to those who hate you, and pray for those who spitefully use you and persecute you, that you may be sons of your Father in heaven; for He makes His sun rise on the evil and on the good, and sends rain on the just and on the unjust.*
> MATTHEW 5:43–48

Jesus doesn't ignore the fact that in a broken world, hate, corruption, and abuse will occur—He clearly states that some people act unjustly toward others. However, He teaches that our response should *contrast* the ugliness in society. For Christians, racial, economic, and gender discrimination are sin and should never exist in homes and churches. When they do, this reveals brokenness on our part—a lack of mind renewal or even the neglect to adopt the New Testament lens about "the other."

Victims Are More Than Statistics

Years ago, an organization called Love INC publicized a need for "mommy helpers." I was able to do housework for a woman in her mid-twenties with two sets of young twins. We had some great conversations, and she became more than a statistic to me. She was a person with a future, someone who needed encouragement and practical assistance.

As young parents facing complicated and costly pregnancies, there were times where Doug and I could not pay for groceries. Every cent needed to go toward medical bills. I tried food stamps, but we were right above the income mark. I hated when creditors would call and harass me. Thankfully, we were in a church community where we could admit our lack without embarrassment. Friends brought bags of groceries to help us in our time of need—I was so thankful.

As Culture Changers, we can put ourselves in others' shoes or remember our humble beginning. Lives are changed when volunteers and employees see the people they serve not as numbers or projects but as neighbors. Community groups, clubs, and churches can take care of their own and also reach out to meet the known needs of those around them.

When will the oppressed go free? When will the "have-nots" have more? It is hard to be patient when we desire to see neighborhoods and schools changed immediately. Many groups have been victims of systemic failures for a long time, and they need a breakthrough now. Our haste to fix the problems often causes us to focus on federal, state, and local programs that can reach people *en masse*. These programs are fine, but the value of one-on-one connection cannot be underestimated. When a person is cared for, encouraged, and valued in the context of a relationship, they can't help but tell other people—they become empowered to serve and encourage others just as they were served and encouraged.

As people find healing, once they are set free from hurts or self-destructive mindsets, they become a weapon and a catalyst. Not a weapon that destroys others—but one that destroys the strongholds and structures entrapping people, families, and communities.

To initiate transformation in the United States at such a level that healing permeates every home and every heart, we need to go deeper and wider than just pressing for new laws, voting, or being a voice for the voiceless. These are good. But the ultimate goal of a Culture Changer is *healing for all.* The oppressed. And the oppressor.

NOTES
3. Lewis, C.S. *Mere Christianity.* Simon & Schuster, 1996., 45.

CHAPTER SIX

A Measuring Stick

Our first teacher is our own heart.
CHEYENNE

My mother used to say to my siblings and me, "The pot can't call the kettle black." In other words, I needed to look at my own weaknesses before I pointed out the failings of others.

Sometimes we excuse our negative habits or behaviors by glibly saying, "Well, I'm just human." Yes, that is true. It is also true that we shouldn't give ourselves a pass if we don't give others a pass.

So far, I have focused largely on race relations in our nation. While this has become a topic that deserves attention, we must be careful not to hold this issue as most important, while matters of male chauvinism and discrimination against women get pushed to the back burner. With this weighty topic, it is tempting to say, "I have not mistreated a woman or someone of another race." Maybe we have not committed adultery but just looked at someone lustfully. There is a measuring stick that puts us all in the same position. Guilty. If we've stood by and watched a scene of harassment, heard an off-color joke and not spoken up, then you—and I, are accomplices.

The "blind eye" of society allowed generations of women to be improperly viewed and misused by generations of men. Female inferiority became a worldview, and male chauvinism was imparted for decades on billboards, through entertainment, and in locker rooms. While the #MeToo movement has raised awareness and empowered women to come together and with one voice to cry, "No more!" the campaign doesn't have the power to change men's thoughts about women. Yes, the outcry can cause a man to think twice before speaking or touching, but by itself, the protest doesn't have the power to stop that man from entertaining thoughts that are demeaning, disrespectful, and repulsive. Deeper change is needed. Wholeness is needed. I believe we've entered a season when God is shaking and shattering the mindset that women are inferior or "made for man." He is working below the surface to reverse this widespread pain in our society, so that hearts change, not just actions.

Thoughts Don't Stay Silent

What we *hear* shapes us and forms our worldview and self-perception. For both men and women, words are powerful; their meanings or inferences can stay in our memories for years and shape our thoughts about ourselves and others. A boy who hears his dad belittle women regularly will be influenced by the older man's words. Similarly, a girl who grows up hearing her mother mock and ridicule men will be shaped by those words.

Both the Hindi teacher Mahatma Gandhi and the Judeo-Christian Bible agree about the power of our thoughts. Despite the inherent differences in these faiths, notice how the following statements reveal a relationship between human thought and behavior:

> *A man is but the product of his thoughts.*
> *What he thinks, he becomes.*
> MAHATMA GANDHI

> *For as he thinks in his heart, so is he.*
> PROVERBS 23:7

Jesus Himself said in Matthew 12:34, "Out of the abundance of the heart the mouth speaks." Gandhi helps to "prove" this reality even for those who don't adhere to Christianity. It may be a hard pill to swallow, but there is a reason Jesus said that any man who thinks about sleeping with a woman in his heart has already done the act; that is the *strength* or *weight* of thought. The human heart is the breeding ground for every adverse action known to humanity. Women will never achieve the status of co-equal beings if they are objectified in the human heart. So the heart is what needs to be healed.

Is there a Hidden Compass for Right and Wrong?

Does our humanity bring with it an unconscious, natural tendency toward good or evil? When we look at the course of human history, that seems to be the case. We can see the good, and we can see the evil. How do we rightly judge what is "good" and what is "evil" when it comes to behavior or a mindset? What is our measuring stick? If we're trying to help others lead a life that is *constructive* rather than *destructive*, we need to be able to discern a situation correctly and make a decision about what is good and what inhibits triune health for that person or society.

As I mentioned earlier, the definition of *shalom* is rightness, completeness, harmony, and wholeness. The opposite is wrongness, incompleteness, dissonance or confusion, and brokenness. It is easy to categorize concepts under the heading of "good," but many of us are reluctant to call something "evil." Sometimes we don't feel comfortable using either categorization, so we lean toward relativism, which is the idea that good or evil is just based on someone's opinion. Relativism says that behavior cannot be called negative or evil because it is subjective to a person's belief system.

Relativism, however, is a worldview based on a faulty lens. Concepts of good and evil cannot be based on one's culture, generation, or opinion. If they are, we lack a foundation—the security that transcends eras, opinions, whims, and assumptions. Imagine how difficult it would be to build a building if everyone used a different length for a meter—one based solely on their opinion. We wouldn't be able to accomplish anything! That illustration is obviously simplistic, but we can apply it on a larger scale to our morals. As a society, we cannot build well unless we use the *same measure*. We have to be on the same page when it comes to what contributes to a productive society and what inhibits it.

As we begin to embrace unseen realities and how we were created, spirit, soul, and body, we end up contemplating questions like these: "Does a person's nature dictate their actions?

How can the same fabric of flesh and blood produce both a Hitler and a Mother Theresa?"

Most people in the world, regardless of their prescribed faith, believe in an invisible dimension that affects the natural world for good or evil. Various religions, philosophers, and skeptics have offered answers for the origin of evil. The Bible teaches that every human being has the capacity to do something good or something that is accepted as being "evil." Moreover, the Bible teaches that evil began before humankind was created—with Lucifer's self-adulation, which God identified and justly punished[4]. Hindus have various schools of thought relating evil to karma, while Buddhists and Muslims have other views. The point is, hundreds of millions of people accept evil as a reality, and humanity must contend with it.

Challenges Along the Way

Our current politically correct culture makes it difficult to call someone's personal beliefs or cultural practices evil, immoral, or unjust. What seems right for one is immoral to another. Around the world, certain religions or governments call for the murder of proselytizers and converts, and they believe they are acting justly as they attack these groups. History offers many examples of people being lynched or killed based on their ethnicity, age, faith, or gender. That was the ideology of Hitler and the Nazis, and one that affected Rwandans, Darfuri citizens, Native Americans in the seventeenth century, and many others.[4] These ideologies are also found in white supremacist organizations.

---

4 Ezekiel 28

It is easy to call something outside of one's culture evil or immoral, but it is not so easy to acknowledge what others have identified as evil or immoral in our own culture. When we embrace the reality of evil—this idea that some behaviors are not right and will never be right—we come face to face with our personal and national history. How do we help someone like the Chinese American father of a baby girl who knows that his parents left their own young daughter to die in the street? He wrestles with guilt and confusion whenever he holds his child and feels the loss of his sister. How do we help the woman of European descent who researches her family history and discovers that some of her ancestors were Native Americans who died on the Trail of Tears? She now has to reconcile two "sides" within her: some of her ancestors were brutal, and some of her ancestors were brutalized. How can she find healing?

All of us need to realize that our history, belief system, and sense of morality are critical to our emotional wholeness. There is an intersection all of us come to where what we believe is morally good meets our personal and family history. In the first example above, the new father will have to decide if the Chinese preference of male babies is ethical. If he decides that killing baby girls because of their gender is immoral, he has to name the belief system that his parents aligned themselves with as evil. While we want to honor our ancestors, many of them did things we don't approve of today. But as we resolve the tension of this intersection, we can move forward into greater wholeness.

Culture Changers help anyone, regardless of how those people look or what they believe or practice. At some point, we will befriend someone going through a life struggle and discover that they endorse things we find repulsive. We can still offer our compassion, insight, and time to help them through their struggle. If we think we have an answer that will help them—but may offend them, we must give them permission to accept or reject whatever we say.

Foundation Determines Course

The world is filled with an array of spiritual beliefs, and as Culture Changers, it can be helpful for us to notice the differences. A person's *foundation*, whatever that foundation is, determines their *course*. Adolf Hitler practiced a form of the occult, and Mother Theresa was a Roman Catholic. Hitler's bent toward evil killed millions of Jews, while Mother Theresa faithfully served the poor. Do some ideologies promote vitality and opportunity more than others? Do some doctrines give a person the freedom to choose their own path? If we believe we were all created on an even playing field, then somewhere along the line, Hitler and Mother Theresa made different choices.

Christianity teaches that humanity suffers from an infection that started with the first man and woman. According to the Genesis story, Adam and Eve disobeyed God; Christians call this sin. Today the term is not politically correct. However, the Hebrew definition of sin, when understood correctly, can help explain the reality of absolute good and absolute evil.

The word *sin* is the Hebrew word *hhatah*, which means missing the mark. Many evangelicals will use the visual analogy of a bull's-eye. If the mark or target is benevolence, altruism, faithfulness, and humility, then sin occurs when our hearts, like arrows, do not hit these virtues. The Bible teaches that Adam and Eve missed the bull's-eye when they disobeyed what God said and did what seemed correct to them instead. They looked at something and elevated their view of that thing above God's command. As a result, everything shifted—their spirits, souls, physical bodies, and even the natural world. The entire earth deviated from God's original course.

This contamination set everything in creation that was previously good on a trajectory toward destruction. The Bible cites sin and this downward trajectory—or curse—as the root cause of disorder, destruction, and suffering. This curse even affected the sperm and ova, the seed of humanity, and therefore we are innately bent toward destructive rather than constructive movement. As humankind populated the earth and formed societies, the curse expanded into every area of human life. So what we see today is just a dim shadow of the natural world's original splendor. Genesis 3 mentions three different curses (or judgments) against humanity, the natural world, and the unseen realm.

This view of sin and free will explains how everyone is born with the capacity to do good and to do harm. Hitler stayed trapped by sin, negative spiritual beliefs, and remained emotionally broken. Millions of people were destroyed by the political system he developed and viewpoints he imparted. Mother Theresa, on the other hand, chose to be a Culture Changer. She walked alongside hurting people, served their practical needs, and prayed for their emotional needs. Although she had moments where, in God's eyes, she missed the mark, her internal bent was to build up, not to tear down.

The Mission to Reestablish Good

Evil abounds. But we can choose to live in such a way that good is reestablished in the earth. To accomplish this mission, we need to recognize that sin is the root that brings turmoil, pain, and injustice in our world.

We also need to see each other through the correct lens. For instance, every white cop needs to be viewed as an individual created in the image of God, and every black male also needs to be seen as an individual created in the image of God. Each struggles with brokenness and is capable of good and evil. Only the release from sin's curse will bring them into their divine purpose. We all have the capacity for good, and we all have the capacity for evil. All of us have sinned and hurt others. All of us are born broken in spirit, soul, and body.

And we all need to be made whole.

NOTES
4. www.endgenocide.org/learn/past-genocides/.

CHAPTER SEVEN

The Merging of Science and the Bible

This most beautiful system of the sun, planets and comets, could only proceed from the counsel and dominion of an intelligent and powerful Being.
Isaac Newton

I love to think of nature as an unlimited broadcasting station, through which God speaks to us every hour, if we will only tune in.
George Washington Carver

My first day of seventh-grade science featured a strange exchange between the teacher and my peers. I don't remember the introductory topic, but our teacher asked us what skin tone humans would eventually have. No one offered a guess. Then he pointed to me and announced that my tan hue would become universal one day. Not only did he believe that we all had the same origin, but he also thought the miscegenation or mixing of ethnicities would never end. I don't remember anything else about that class. His statement made me conclude that science carried evidence of creationism.

I grew up in a community where belief in creationism was normal. I don't remember learning about evolution until junior high school or high school. At that point, natural science and the Bible became opposites. But after being introduced to microevolution, quantum physics, and microbiology as an adult, I realized they weren't opposites at all. When it comes to how we are created, natural science and the Bible support each other.

New research in genetics and brain science offers answers to the root of personal challenge, family and generational dysfunction, and community turmoil. To have a holistic view of human brokenness, we can look to these topics and spiritual belief—and learn why the pathway to wholeness takes time.

Personal Challenges and DNA

Do you know a veteran who has post-traumatic stress disorder? Upon return to their homes, some American soldiers experience this because of the horrors they see and the painful decisions they're trained to make. Likewise, victims of rape, terrorism, and natural disasters can experience levels of PTSD. The National Center for PTSD sites any life-threatening experience as a precipitator of this condition.[5]

Science is uncovering reasons for human behavior that need to be considered in our quest to help groups of people. When a large group of individuals of the same ethnicity or nationality experience continued trauma on the scale of American slavery or Native American displacement, transgenerational trauma and cultural PTSD are terms that describe the ongoing effects that prevent them from moving forward.

These forms of PTSD affect our genes. Epigenetic memory can also be called *inherited memory* or *biological memory*. The biblical word for sins that repeat themselves in a family line is iniquity, and epigenetic memory explains how iniquity works. The idea that "we turn into our parents" one day is humorous but factual.

In our genes are embedded responses to a variety of situations. When we look at a community or people group where certain unhealthy behaviors are common, it is vital to consider epigenetics and, in so doing, begin digging into unseen parts of our composition: the spirit, soul, and DNA.

Epigenetic memory is what happens when an individual's mental and emotional processes produce chemical reactions in their cells. These chemical reactions can be imprinted on our DNA and, when that happens, be passed on to our children through meiosis. In other words, people living today might be carrying the pain, fear, and resentment—and prejudice of their ancestors.

Dr. Caroline Leaf, a South African Cognitive Neuroscientist, specializes in metacognitive and cognitive neuropsychology. She spends a lot of time discussing the topic of transgenerational epigenetic inheritance. I first saw her on a Christian broadcast, and her research has come to play a significant role in how I pray for people. She has found that circumstances and thought patterns in one generation can be "deposited" in the egg and sperm cells, which means *future* generations actually carry these memories in their DNA.

...the studies on epigenetics show us that the good, the bad, and the ugly do come down through the generations, but your mind is the signal—the epigenetic factor—that switches these genes on or off.[6]

Right there is the explanation for why families can find themselves trapped in the same unhealthy patterns for generations. We can't just blame human will—the root goes deeper.

But Dr. Leaf does more than just point out this issue. Her research also shows how we can stop being affected by predispositions—the answer is to renew our minds[5]. Dr. Leaf calls this renewing process "directed mind input" or neuroplasticity.

Family traits can be subtle. My son saw my dad only a few times in his life, but strangely, my son has the same intonation as my dad did—the same pauses and vocal timbre. I now believe this is the result of epigenetic memory coming through my DNA. It is a matter of genes and their chemistry. Whether a gene is active or not can depend on chemical compounds that click onto the DNA structure, toggling the gene's on-off switch (think of it as a biological lock and key). These changes can be clicked into place—and *they can also be undone*. Environment and lifestyle can influence gene activity.[7]

A vast amount of scholarly information can be found about epigenetic memory through the National Institutes of Health website and other medical journals. Twin studies have been a useful tool in understanding how cognitive memories

---

5 Romans 12:2 Do not conform to the pattern of this world, but be transformed by the renewing of your mind.

of one generation can be transferred to another generation. Dr. Leaf's research also supports twin studies.

> Epigenetic changes represent a biological response to an environmental signal. That response can be inherited through the generations via the epigenetic marks. But if you remove the signal, the epigenetic marks will fade.[8]

What are the signals that perpetuate these markers? For those of us who have identified negative generational predispositions—or as some call them, *generational curses*—it is helpful to be aware of possible signals. Why? Because when the signals are undone, the epigenetic marks fade. When listening to family stories, if we discover events that initiated a grandmother's depression or an uncle's suicide, we can do the soul work and prayer needed to not be triggered the same way they were—that is, we can remove the platform on which the signals land. This way, we can maintain our hope and freedom should we ever find ourselves facing similar events or circumstances in our lifetime.

Could war, racial tensions, or divorce be a signal for some of us? Is the presence of these things in society a sign not just of our present brokenness but of the brokenness of past generations?

I understand how this idea—unknown signals causing hidden generational dysfunctions which then trigger our reactions—could make people nervous. But we don't have to respond in worry or fear. We can encourage ourselves and anyone we walk alongside that, no matter what, inherited patterns can be undone, as Dr. Leaf says. As we move toward triune wholeness, we naturally cause known or unknown environmental signals to weaken in their influence. Here is one "small" example: pushing through marital discord to avoid divorce goes a long way for families where divorce has become generational. In a later chapter we'll discuss spiritual factors that undo epigenetic influences as well.

Generational Healing

The fact that families can be healed from iniquity (repeated sins in a family line) is exciting—our family systems can end unhealthy cycles. Embracing this reality will help us as we walk alongside people who come into our lives. We will need to be patient because healing takes time, and we can empathize because we are on the same journey of healing.

Environmental epigenetic researchers look at everything from climate, pollutants, nutrition, to other potentially stress-inducing factors and how these factors affect DNA. People can inherit weaknesses from anxiety to near-sightedness. Positive predispositions are passed down as well. For example, leadership skills, musical giftedness, or analytical skills can pass down a family line. Like iniquity, these traits and propensities are also carried through our DNA.

A curse is a biblical term for a tendency toward destructive rather than constructive movement. As stated earlier, it is a consequence of sin. Although the human soul is intangible, anything from pride to the fear of failure and even a propensity toward financial lack can be carried through DNA. Compounded by environmental factors and family culture, these propensities can stay deeply rooted within a person or culture. A curse—this tendency is one reason communities remain in a mode of deterioration for generations.

There is some evidence that different types of environmental stimuli can alter the epigenome of the whole brain or related neural circuits, contributing to long-lasting behavioral phenotypes that may be transmitted from parent to offspring via transgenerational mechanisms.[9]

Consider a family where low self-esteem is an inherited predisposition. If that family uses name-calling in a moment of conflict, the self-esteem issue will stay entrenched. Unknowingly, they have normalized it for yet another generation. They have "cursed" their children through name-calling. Negative words destroy a person's self-image and affect cognitive and emotional development. This is one reason some students don't do well in school. The tendencies of their family system or home environment inhibit their wellbeing, which in turn affects their ability to learn.

Awareness brings the possibility of change. As family members acknowledge their weaknesses, coping mechanisms, and inherited sin patterns, they can progress into triune health. Being open about the struggles of one generation allows the next generation to see their parents' resolve as they embrace change.

Epigenetic memory opens up a whole new world for us all. Every ethnic group is affected by the negative behaviors, thought patterns, and propensities of their ancestors. The problem of broken families, absentee fathers, and children out of wedlock can be attributed to the curse of slavery, which handicapped millions of African Americans for two hundred years. Many issues that African Americans face are due to post-traumatic slave syndrome. African Americans, whose female ancestors were raped by white slave owners, carry predispositions—good and bad, from their European and African bloodlines. And for them, this reality of carrying the DNA of the oppressor is infuriating.

When we consider epigenetic memory, we realize that politics, education, and economics can do only so much. They cannot bring corporate wholeness and freedom from inherited trauma. While programs and incentives can help alleviate the practical challenges African Americans face, triune healing will bring this group from internal struggle into total victory.

Culture Changers who have relationships with the descendants of slaves *or other people groups* who've suffered from systemic oppression need to understand that epigenetic factors can be triggered every day through signals—incidents of police brutality to billboards to the absence of a father. Inherited memories from eras of colonialism, slavery, and war will trigger mistrust, anger, and fear. What can we do? We can help these individuals by explaining the triggers and guiding them through the healing process, which includes understanding spiritual realities, renewing their minds, and forgiving others. For the African American community, remembering the testimonies of the descendants of slaves—Martin Luther King Jr., George Washington Carver, Benjamin Banneker, women like Katherine Johnson and Condoleezza Rice, and learning about Africans like the Bible figure Niger and the theologian Augustine—motivates and evokes vision. When coupled with other tools that help bring about health and wellbeing, triune healing can actually occur on a corporate level.

When it comes to prejudice and racism, *all* of us need to consider the inherited memories and predispositions that influence our opinions about other people.

Quantum Physics and Spiritual Belief

The world of science and spiritual belief are merging. Research is confirming what various practitioners of spiritual and emotional healing have known for years: each part of our triune composition (spirit, soul, and body) affects and is affected by the others. We're triune beings, and as we see where the spirit, soul, and body overlap, we're better prepared to live as our Creator intended.

You may have learned, like me, that science is valid because it is empirical, while belief or faith is ethereal. Although the dichotomy of Darwinian evolution and biblical creationism cause many people to think that faith and science are incompatible, scientific concepts exist throughout Scripture. The truth is, both are tangible if you believe that the unseen world is a higher reality than the visible world.

Science helps us define and understand our existence. Many believe that science is the revelation of the Creator's genius, but whether we believe in an intelligent designer we call *God* or not, human DNA reveals a common point of origin. The sciences can be thought of as man's attempt to give comprehension to the form, purpose, and boundaries of humanity and the natural world. Various religions support the validity of science when it comes to spiritual belief.

All religions, arts, and sciences are branches of the same tree.

ALBERT EINSTEIN

Max Planck, German physicist and 1918 Nobel Prize recipient, is known for making quantum physics a valid academic course of study. A 2019 Encyclopedia Britannica article written by Roger Stuewer quotes Planck describing his pursuit of physics:

> Original decision to devote myself to science was a direct result of the discovery...that the laws of human reasoning coincide with the laws governing the sequences of the impressions we receive from the world about us; ...outside world is something independent from man, something absolute, and the quest for the laws which apply to this absolute appeared...as the most sublime scientific pursuit in life.[10]

Planck was a man who attempted to influence Nazi leadership to pursue a constructive rather than a destructive course when it came to the Jewish race. Stuewer writes:

> In his later years, Planck devoted more and more of his writings to philosophical, aesthetic, and religious questions...Planck went directly to Hitler in an attempt to reverse Hitler's devastating racial policies...[11]

Quantum physics uncovers many unseen processes that govern not only our physical body but the immaterial parts of us. The Bible uses words like *light* and *sound* that explain the effects of divine power in the earth and the benefit of aligning ourselves with our Creator.

God is Light, and in Him there is no darkness at all.
JOHN 1:5

Planck's discovery that light emits energy corresponds with the Bible verse that says within God resides the power that created everything. Power or energy is a part of His essence. John 1:4 reads, "In Him was life [and the power to bestow life], and the life was the Light of men." The word *light* means goodness, purity, and order—and it also speaks of the divine energy that creates and sustains. Even some Hindi beliefs agree with the areas of our triune composition as explained by Scripture. For example, while Chakra affirmations counter biblical doctrine, the various anatomical zones (areas of the human body) are merely energy centers.

I can understand how showing a similarity between two opposing faiths may trouble many people, but if you believe in one Creator, then all human beings can perceive clues about how we were created yet translate or steward them differently.

C. S. Lewis writes in *Mere Christianity:*

> If you are a Christian, you do not have to believe that all the other religions are simply wrong all through. If you are an atheist, you do have to believe that the main point in all the religions of the world is simply one huge mistake. If you are a Christian, you are free to think that all these religions, even the queerest ones, contain at least some hint of truth.[12]

The differences are the result of sin. The Bible teaches that because of sin, we discern truth through a skewed or darkened lens. When it comes to quantum physics and spiritual faith, some people may use the idea of energy fields in and around us in a way that skews the Creator's intent, but at the same time, others may use energy in a way that satisfies God's purpose for it. The journey toward wholeness gives us the ability to get clarity—to understand and steward the processes of creation according to God's will.

Then Jesus spoke to them again, saying, "I am the light of the world. He who follows Me shall not walk in darkness but have the light of life." (John 8:12)

The biblical view of light as a symbol of goodness, purity, and alignment with the Creator is also found in other spiritual beliefs. As referenced previously, the differences between Christianity and Hinduism are vast, but both validate that the human spirit is real and active. Contemplative prayer and centering meditation differ only in the focus of spiritual engagement. All types of biblical prayer focus on a benevolent Creator and Redeemer, whereas spiritual centering promotes "mindfulness," which is a conscious tuning-in to oneself within one's surroundings. Both belief systems recognize that as triune beings, we must allow times to "be" in a posture of rest and quietness.

Meditate in your heart upon your bed and be still.
(Psalm 4:4 NASB)

Be still and know that I am God. (Psalms 46:10 NLT)

The main difference between these methods of achieving spiritual rest is an acknowledgment of the Creator versus a focus on ourselves—the created. Finding the common intersections of various faiths can be helpful when we are in relationships with other people who have different beliefs and life experiences.

Healing culture involves layers of issues and levels of our humanity that many of us have never understood. Peering in to examine how we were created to function and then zooming out to see how individual wholeness affects society helps us see why we have to persevere. Change won't happen overnight. But we can take the first step.

NOTES:
5. National Center for PTSD | Understanding PTSD and PTSD Treatment, ptsd.va.gov May 2019.

6. Leaf, Caroline. *Switch on Your Brain.* p. 58

7. "(c) 2018 Erika Hayasaki, as first published in *The Atlantic.*"

8. Leaf, Dr. Caroline. *Switch on Your Brain,* p. 59

9. Schuebel, Kornel et al. "Making Sense of Epigenetics." *The international journal of neuropsychopharmacology* vol. 19,11 pyw058. 15 Jun. 2016, doi:10.1093/ijnp/pyw058

10. Stuewer, Roger H. "Max Planck." *Encyclopædia Britannica,* Encyclopædia Britannica, Inc., 19 Apr. 2019, www.britannica.com/biography/Max-Planck.

11. Ibid.,

12. Lewis, C. S. *Mere Christianity.* Simon & Schuster, 1996., 43

CHAPTER EIGHT

Caught in the Web of Systems

Our society is a complex maze of interwoven mechanisms. These mechanisms control how we live and do business. Where our food comes from and the prices that we pay. From the time we are born, our medical records, places of residence, and ethnic identity dictate everything from where we go to school to what opportunities are offered to us. Many mechanisms are necessary—banking, food distribution, education, law enforcement—but too often, we are subject to their failures. Bribery. Cronyism. Embezzlement. Corruption often continues when it should be dismantled. Many individuals and families become Ping-Pong balls tossed about by restrictive policies and political agendas instead of receiving the simple, down-to-earth help they need. What is our role in the undoing?

Let us take a deeper look at *why* corruption and broken systems continue.

Mindsets Rule the World

The actions of those in power will affect everyone within the realm of their authority, and unless those in power align themselves with the Creator's intents, negative mindsets and soul issues will rule their behavior. The head of a human resources department can believe that all people are created equal yet endorse higher pay for men, stating that women are more likely to take time off for maternity leave or family needs. But according to a biblical perspective, a laborer—any laborer, male or female—is worthy of the work they do, and God is no respecter of persons.

To further point out how mindsets affect societal systems, let's look at the topic of population control. Some believe that population control is a valid issue. Climate change, food shortages, and unwanted pregnancies make ideas like child limits or mandatory sterilization worthwhile. According to this mindset, controlling or limiting population growth across the globe would help extend the life of the earth's resources and protect the natural environment from overuse. Those who embrace this mindset likely view their solutions as constructive, while others see these solutions as destructive because they eliminate individual liberty and assert that the value of being alive is based on a certain quality of life.

Belief is powerful and often based on personal experience. It is firm and usually unyielding. For those who believe that we, as human beings, secure our destiny, population control is reasonable. Abortion and assisted suicide are reasonable. Efforts to foster self-preservation at the expense of others, to control human lifespans, and to hinder the movement and prosperity of people seem reasonable if one believes that humanity has the right to determine its course.

So as you can see, since systems are built and overseen by people, many of the systems and mechanisms in place are *destructive* to individual health and prosperity, simply because they were created by men and women whose mindsets are not aligned with the Creator's intent. In these cases, it is not just the "masses" who suffer—it is also those who shape and steer these systems. Their mindset of fear and control keeps them bound to their brokenness.

As we navigate this maze, we will likely uncover rules and regulations that are unfair to the people we are trying to help. Also, the political, economic, and social dynamics that influence how and why organizations—particularly large organizations—function can be challenging to figure out.

When deciding which organizations or companies to support or what systems need change, here are two questions a Culture Changer may ask:

1) What does this organization support, and what do they do that leads to individual freedom and wellness, family prosperity, and community opportunity?

2) Does the outworking of their mission or this system maintain or decrease personal brokenness, family dysfunction, and community chaos?

Stewarding Progress

Globalism and job security have changed the dynamics of family life in the last fifty to sixty years. Generally speaking, people move wherever they can to find a good job. As a result, relatives no longer live in the same neighborhoods or even in the same state. Disengaged neighbors are also a by-product of our economic system. People move in, and people move out. Employees and college students alike, who are in a location for a short time, are often not concerned about investing themselves in their locality as much as focusing on their own pursuits. This is a consumer mentality versus an investment mentality. But those who see relationships as a worthy investment—one of giving and receiving, sacrifice, and growth—will make a positive impact no matter how long they live in a locality.

Due to this consumer mentality, many cities have seen neighborhoods slowly crumble, and the remaining residents fall prey to many symptoms of hopelessness like drugs and crime. Sometimes, gentrification occurs, which adds to the hopelessness, bitterness, and resentment in those who live in that area.

Progress involves movement, while stagnancy limits growth and experience. Therefore, change can be a blessing or a curse. As a society, we need to recognize the systems and even trends that are destructive to people's overall wellness. Technological trends have changed the way we connect. We tend to communicate via texting and online platforms more frequently than going over and knocking on our neighbor's door. The economic, judicial, housing, and other systems are not evil in and of themselves; they just need to be stewarded in a way that promotes prosperity, opportunity, and personal wellness for all. We need ingenuity and a heart to invest in the wellbeing of others.

In the late nineteenth century, cotton brought wealth, but it also depleted the land of nutrients. As a result of human greed, the soil of the American South became malnourished. But George Washington Carver, a former slave who became a world-famous scientist and inventor, introduced the concept of crop rotation, which replenished the fertility of the soil.

Where did this solution come from?

The solution came as a simple idea he had after praying in what he called "God's Little Workshop" or his laboratory. If we seek God, we can receive ideas on how to restore the necessary systems to be life-giving. Carver was gifted with a love for science, which is how God used him to fix a broken agricultural system. How we are wired will dictate the role we play in repairing what is broken.

Rescuing Individual Destinies

It is unfair to put people in boxes. We need to dismantle our opinions of others based on what we believe they represent. When we acknowledge a person's independence and ability to think for themselves, we have a better chance of seeing why they're alive—the unique purpose of their existence and how they are meant to influence the world around them.

We are taught to categorize, such as when we have to fill out a form. Often we are asked to check a box to indicate our *race*. Unfortunately, the word race, as we use it, is an unfair category—a social construct that groups ethnicities according to four controversial racial classifications. Instead, there should be dozens of boxes, from which we can check the ethnic mixture of our ancestry.

We all do it—we categorize the world around us and build a framework we can use to help us think and communicate. Often, we group people according to physical characteristics, traditions, language, and geographical location. But another way we arrange people is through social circles: churchgoers, employers, liberals, academics, etc. Unfortunately, we can unintentionally limit people by only associating them with a specific group—one that we view through stereotypes. Also, some individuals who build and manage our systems—economic, educational, political, etc. use these categories in ways that undermine a person's progress.

Our mission is to release individuals into the wholeness that brings unlimited possibilities for their lives. In doing so, we must encourage them to find out *what* they believe and *why*. Have they deliberately determined their worldview, or have they taken on the ideas of those around them in order to belong? The tendency for *groupthink* naturally occurs when people adopt the ideas of their preferred social group. Because of the legitimate emotional need to belong, we all do this. Then we get comfortable with our views, which are normalized by our environment.

For this reason, some families, communities, and social groups have more difficulty eradicating destructive patterns than others because of the sheer number of people who think the same way. Their view has become a *stronghold*. But as people discover their divine purpose—their distinctiveness, they will need to dispose of any thinking patterns that oppose their individual destiny. Geroge Washington Carver had to do this as he pursued a course that few former slaves would.

The Need for Individuality and Independence

Many people grow up feeling like their family system, friends, or community members encroach upon their individuality. Family pride or loyalty can teach children that their *heritage* trumps individual distinctiveness.

I coined the term *tri-jurisdictional healing* to mean how the healing of individuals progresses to the healing of families and communities. Each of these divine jurisdictions—the individual, the family, and the community—has distinct boundaries and unique purposes. Although these jurisdictions naturally overlap, sometimes one jurisdiction will attempt to control or exert unhealthy influence over the others. This is important to recognize because two jurisdictions (the family and community) have an impact that outlives one person's lifetime through groupthink and epigenetics.

Personhood Establishes Your Role in a Bigger Story

Sometimes, when a person assimilates into a different social group or cultural group, they are criticized because their new circle thinks and lives differently from their groups of origin—family system, faith circle, or neighborhood. The original group can feel abandoned, dishonored, or judged. But autonomy—the freedom to be *you*—is critical to a healthy sense of self. Each of us has a responsibility to follow the specific purpose and path designed by the Creator before we were born, regardless of the family, community, or culture we were born into. I often wondered why God led my husband and me to homeschool and attend churches where most of the members were white. We didn't mind, but it is not easy to be "the only." We learned to keep our hearts and minds open and accept that God had a unique plan and a specific perspective He wanted us to gain.

Our sense of self or personhood is often affected by external factors or relational associations. These should not supercede our core identity which was established by God before we were born. C. S. Lewis articulated it this way:

What I call my "self" now is hardly a person at all. It's mainly a meeting place for various natural forces, desires, and fears, etcetera, some of which come from my ancestors, and some from my education, some perhaps from devils. The self you were really intended to be is something that lives not from nature but from God.[13]

The Declaration of Independence is correct—we are created equally. Each of us is like a fingerprint: original and unique. As autonomous beings, male or female, we are created in His image. His intent for relationships begins with the family. After that, our sphere of influence expands as we discern our life's purpose. Wherever we go, we are charged to work together in a universal story that is bigger than any era or generation.

Moments That Define Purpose

Harriet Tubman is an American hero. Her desire to be free evolved into a mission to see as many slaves escape the system of slavery as possible. As a result, she put her life on the line time after time and extended her hand toward others even when her life was in danger. It wasn't enough for her to experience freedom—she wanted others to experience it as well. Abolitionists named her after Moses because of her mission to set people free.

In the Old Testament, Moses experienced a series of defining moments to discover his real identity and divine purpose. Before he led the enslaved Israelites out of Egypt, he had to introduce himself to them. They had known him only as a prince of Egypt. Establishing his identity meant also returning to his Egyptian family and telling them that he had discovered his true bloodline. Once his identity was acknowledged, the cultural identity of Israel was established, and this people group was able to fulfill their unique purpose in the Earth.

My point is that casting off limiting strongholds paves the way for people to discover their uniquely created divine purpose. Within that purpose are seasonal assignments— job, ministry, volunteerism—which can fluctuate over a lifetime, but each will complement an individual's personality and gifting.

A career is simply a means to accomplish part of our purpose, which centers in human interaction. A teacher imparts not only academic knowledge and a love for learning but also character and worldview. A business owner can impact her employees and demonstrate a healthy work ethic of diligence and integrity. Engineers find better ways for us to function on the planet. Any career can be used to foster tri-jurisdictional healing.

In their chosen field, both employer and employee can make decisions that benefit others. From friendships to the hands-on processes of the job, both can have an impact that produces a healthy work environment for themselves as well as make systems and products grounded in integrity and excellence.

As I mentioned previously, George Washington Carver, had a divine purpose whose impact touched the entire agricultural system of the South. By changing the *system*, he provided the means for individuals to prosper. His inventiveness transformed the economy of the South during his lifetime.

There is a simple litmus test we can employ to determine whether or not a person is fulfilling their divine purpose. This litmus test is not meant to judge, but to discern where any person is—from political leader to parent— in their journey towards wholeness. *Is their life's pursuit constructive or destructive for the people around them?* We are here to walk in health and freedom and divine purpose—and to help others do the same.

NOTES
13. "C. S. Lewis Quotes." BrainyQuote.com. BrainyMedia Inc, 2019. 18 May 2019.

CHAPTER NINE

Repairing the Family

Call it a clan, call it a network, call it a tribe, call it a family:
Whatever you call it, whoever you are, you need one.[14]
JANE HOWARD

Connection breeds life. This statement is more than just a biological truth—it's one we can feel. We actually need to be connected to each other in healthy ways so we can prosper.

Connection, or lack thereof, becomes a part of a family's culture. That culture is also based on the attitudes, traditions, and worldview of the parents and guardians, plus emotional dispositions, inherited behaviors, racial background, and environment; all those things can affect the culture of a family. When a family fails to provide the connection that God intended, members look to fulfill those needs in other relationships. Friendship can offer a connection that is often more satisfying than one's own family relationships. As some say,

"You can't pick your family," meaning that we often wish we could!

However, despite how rewarding friendships can be, God's intent is for the family to be our first healthy connection. Ironically, even though family dysfunction can permeate generations, a blood connection brings a profound sense of identity, where physical characteristics, talents, and history are the highlights. Nevertheless, any unmet emotional connection from our family of origin is a soul wound that needs to be healed.

Family systems are the building block of communities. Without family identity, we become a collection of individuals whose connectivity is based only on our humanity—a connection far too remote and expansive to appeal to our need for closeness, accessibility, and the ability to relate to shared experiences and daily living. We are wired to be known intimately. Every mother knows their child better than that child knows themselves during the developmental years. During adolescence, we become more aware of our innate emotional and physical longing for intimacy. Our sense of worth develops in an intimate setting. A family—even adopted family, offers a sense of home and a shared environment, even if it is a stressful one.

With the obvious importance of the family in mind, we can consider the divine purpose of the family—it's "function," according to sociologists. The functions of a family are primarily "reproduction; socialization; care, protection, and emotional support; assignment of status; and regulation of sexual behavior through social norms."[15]

Nowadays—with the intensifying conversation about societal paradigm shifts, racial divisiveness, economic class systems, divorce, and even gender politics—many people think about the family structure through a paradigm called the *conflict perspective*. This perspective views the family structure as a force that promotes male dominance and economic inequalities (due to inherited social status).[16] Conflict theorists don't see the divine purpose in the family structure—they believe it is simply a social construct.

So as Culture Changers, we need to analyze our view of the significance of the family. What does the family mean? Why does it exist? What is its divine purpose? However, we can answer these questions correctly *only* from a place of emotional health—not emotional brokenness. Open wounds will skew our viewpoint. To one degree or another, all of us have experienced hurt within our homes. Some of our experiences were extremely traumatic. Some of us grew up never knowing our parents due to death, prison, or abandonment. Unhealed trauma can cause us to *discount* God's desire for family. Our ears only hear our pain, not God's plan.

But despite these experiences, we must acknowledge the good things God wanted for us in the family structure. Then we need to grieve our loss.

Hurt Begets Hurt

Over coffee one morning, a college friend shared with me that when she was growing up, the children were shooed away from the adults and told to play by themselves. This custom occurred regularly at extended family gatherings. As a result, more than one child, in more than one generation, was molested by an older cousin.

In this case, the family structure leaned toward exclusion and neglect, which resulted in limited physical protection and emotional security. "Go play by yourselves" was the family norm that became a "curse," if you will, buried deep within the family culture. Once my friend understood the curse and acknowledged its effects, the cycle shattered in her life. She established her freedom by grieving her trauma and forgiving her abuser. Part of her healing process also included gathering two generations of sisters, nieces, and cousins for a weekend retreat, where she provided for them a safe space of vulnerability, sharing, and prayer. Nothing remained hidden. Wellbeing comes from transparency and freedom, while affliction comes from secrecy and bondage. That is what the Bible teaches, and we see it play out again and again in our lives.

Whether they realize it or not, parents and guardians direct their child's triune health. Healthy families have a "push and pull," a releasing and securing, which helps their children grow. The *push* comes when it is time for children to grow into another stage of responsibility, freedom, and autonomy. This time comes according to the child's maturity and isn't based on the parents' desire for convenience. The *pull*[6] has the power to show children that they are adored, desired, and belong. It isn't selfish or stifling. Both the push and the pull maintain the security of the relationship and the value of change. The family in the last story did not operate the "push" correctly.

Knowledge brings power. Now equipped with the understanding that this family norm was not healthy, these adult women were able to go home and change how their family gatherings were done. Now they can encourage other adult

---

6 Act of drawing someone physically or emotionally close to affirm love and security. See my book, *Cultivating the Souls of Parents*, p.162-163

relatives to include and help supervise the kids. These changes will sow seeds of security and safety into a new generation. The actions of the women in this family reflect their new understanding and a heart change that will end the cycle.

One person's healing can begin a chain reaction to family transformation. Self-awareness, emotional honesty, and humility create and maintain a quality of health in families. The healthier the parent, the better able they will be to equip their children to navigate their own life episodes and healing journeys. Families that consider their genetic and emotional lineages can go a step further and pinpoint *past* dysfunctional thinking that has led to *current* unhealthy behaviors. Then they can help bring healing by making necessary changes.

A common phrase in healing circles is "hurting people hurt people." Many of us carry unresolved pain from the trauma we experienced in our homes—any trauma, not just specific kinds of trauma. However, we can recognize and subsequently *break* every curse and undo the unfavorable conditions we were born into. When a generation of family members trade unhealthy patterns for healthy ones, they offer an awareness of the family's prior brokenness and enable the next generation to live free of it. They become able to train the next generation in those healthy patterns.

When we consider situations where the same sin reappears generation after generation, and then consider the storyline of human history, we see that the effects of sin in Genesis 3 are long term and wide-ranging. But our stories can end in triumph. As we move toward wholeness, we connect with God and others in a way that releases redemption and healing.

Is Parenting Undermined?

Articles on parenting styles—practical for some and controversial for others—have been published by news sources from the Associated Press to Common Sense Media. Sometimes perspectives that devalue parenting and undermine a parent's authority are touted in the name of child advocacy. Even the famous phrase "It takes a village" enforces a worldview that childrearing is *corporate* work, but this mindset comes subtly close to crossing the divine boundaries between the jurisdiction of family and community—or family and the "state." Raising kids is the sole responsibility of parents or legal guardians. Sure, parents and guardians can delegate and resource other people to assist where needed, but a parent's authority always remains.

That is a painful reality in the face of horror stories about parental neglect and abuse. Human brokenness will always lead to tragedy. It is good that the number of abusive parents pales in comparison to the number of parents who provide physical security and emotional support to their children, but even so, we need to ask some questions as a nation. How do we protect abused children through legislation without infringing on the rights of parents who are not harming their children? But the first question we should ask is, *how* do we define "bad parent"?

Most of us would say that a "bad parent" is one who causes physical harm and danger to their child. However, some indigenous and Middle Eastern cultures practice genital mutilation and child marriage; these acts are part of their culture, and the parents don't recognize these practices as abuse. What do we think of them? Similarly, giving children puberty blockers to limit the manifestation of their biological gender is considered mental and emotional abuse by some doctors and psychiatrists. So what is actual "child abuse," and what is not?

Though a Culture Changer can come alongside people who live and think differently than we do, a line will need to be drawn that delineates good from evil. But who is responsible for designating what is good and what is evil? Whose voice wins? For example, some may say that Christian children are taught gender identity discrimination. Could that be defined as abuse? If so, then millions of Christian parents—even Muslim parents could lose their divine right to raise their children according to their prescribed spiritual belief system.

Today we see a plethora of parenting views and family lifestyle choices. Many transgender parents feel threatened by evangelical parents who don't want schools to teach that same-sex marriage is acceptable. This public debate shows the problem that arises when different measuring sticks are used to determine what is moral and healthy. Each side would say that the others are "bad parents," not them.

In the past, educational systems or child advocacy groups with a statist bent have trumped the importance of the family of origin. As a result, parental rights groups were birthed to empower parents to maintain the boundaries of jurisdictional authority when it comes to their children. Does the jurisdiction of the community or state need to respect the sovereignty of the family—no matter the worldview the family embraces? In the name of individual freedom and family identity, do we, as a society, need to accept that differences will always exist and no community, state, or federal system has the right to define what is "bad" or "unhealthy" for children?

But here I think is the main question—the question that sums up the focus of this book. As Culture Changers, let's help people get to a point where they can ask themselves, "Is my belief system conducive to constructive movement and triune health, or is it conducive to destructive movement and continued brokenness?" Once people can start asking that question honestly, they will begin to gravitate toward certain principles that bring health and healing over the long haul.

New Era, New Challenges

Parenting today is no easy feat. Nearly across the board, parents face issues today that no previous generation has. Ron Taffel's article, "The Decline and Fall of Parental Authority and What Therapists Can Do About It" mentions something called "parent-blame," which he explains as:

> the tendency on the part of child experts, including too often me, to blame parents for what's going on. In fact, as I speak with child clinicians and educators across the country, the parent-blame knocks me over. I can't help but think, How can we help the very parents we seem to hold in such disdain? It seems particularly ironic that, as therapists, we don't appear to have empathy for parents who are trying to muddle through a perfect storm of interconnected cultural and social circumstances that undermine the foundations of parental self-confidence and integrity, even of family life itself.[17]

A Culture Changer needs to understand that all human beings, from the child expert to the teacher to the parent, are broken. Even professionals can act on faulty assumptions. Taffel's point addresses this. We need to be careful not to assume that a child advocate, a judge, a protective services employee, or a foster parent is somehow wiser or more "whole" than the birth parent. That is just not true, because we're all dealing with brokenness in different ways. Obviously, this doesn't mean that a physically abused child should remain in the abusive home. What it means is that society cannot say that the "experts" know how to meet the needs of a child *best*. A Culture Changer who understands the situation—the layers of individual brokenness, the value of family health, and how these first two jurisdictions (the individual and family) can bring forth transformed communities—will seek to strengthen every family of origin versus undermine its original purpose.

This tri-jurisdictional process of healing and transformation is long term. It will take decades, perhaps two or three generations, to right a point of pain inside an individual, family, and community. Not everything can be fixed at once, but the good news is it *can* be fixed.

Another challenge today has to do with humanistic ideals. This ideology proposes that humankind can achieve perfection and fulfillment without God's assistance. It uplifts human ingenuity and discards divine dependence. As a result, many parents strive for the ideal child or family based on popular trends. Finding the best parenting strategies and the best education that leads to the best college is "in style." This emphasis tends to be found among those with above-average incomes. Medical technology supports this mindset by offering the capability to "order up a child" according to a menu of preferences. These designer children are viewed by biomedical ethics professionals as the children of the future—products of fertility clinics and gene editing.

Nearly every parent has some kind of desire for the "ideal child," whatever that looks like to them. Someone who takes after the mother or father. Someone kind, loving, or talented in a particular area. But whatever the parent's desire, being a parent is meant to be a role built on selflessness and a relationship with another person who is alive for a purpose far beyond the parents' goals.

As parents start realizing their own generational and individual brokenness, raising another generation can feel daunting, perhaps even undesirable. As Culture Changers, we can come alongside parents and encourage them to stay fixed on the *process*, not merely the goal. Just as obtaining individual wholeness is a difficult yet beautiful process, so is parenting and family repair.

NOTES

14. Jane Howard, *Life* Magazine

15. *OpenStax CNX*, cnx.org/contents/M_RkLtXv@2/The-Three-Sociological-Paradigms-Perspectives.

16. Ibid.

17. "The Decline And Fall Of Parental Authority." *Psychotherapy Networker,* www.psychotherapynetworker.org/magazine/article/287/the-decline-and-fall-of-parental-authority.

CHAPTER TEN

Understanding How Sin Affects the Earth

Hate the sin, love the sinner.
MAHATMA GANDHI

Sin turned the world upside down. Instead of magnifying our Creator and functioning from His design, we became wired to discard and deny His relevance. Since the day Adam and Eve ate from the forbidden tree, sin's infection has affected every generation of humanity.

In this chapter, I will define sin, offer the solution, and discuss how people may react to the solution, which centers around *who* the Creator is and *what* He did for humankind.

As stated earlier, many evangelicals use the analogy of a bull's-eye to describe sin because the Hebrew word means "to miss the mark."[7] Adam and Eve missed the bull's-eye. The Creator's instruction was dismissed—they reasoned within themselves based on what they saw and what another created being suggested. So the first man and woman went from a state of shalom, through the door of disobedience, and found themselves bound by sin—a power that spread throughout the natural world. We can describe it as an *infection*.

Since each of us is affected by this infection, so is every culture and nation. Sin—a continual *missing the mark*—skews our perceptions and, therefore, taints every idea and endeavor in history. According to our Creator's standard, we are "not on point." Or we're "a bit off." While we can recognize glimpses of divine goodness in history, we can also see the distortions caused by sin. Tribal division in Africa, male chauvinism in Asian and Middle Eastern cultures, Spanish machismo, European lust for domination—all of these things were birthed in Adam and Eve's misfire.

We've talked about inherited memory and the scientific explanation it offers for how iniquity continued after the Flood, where all but eight people were wiped out. The effects of Genesis 3—when Adam and Eve ate the forbidden fruit—coursed its way through history and permeated every individual, family, and community. But the good news is—it's a course that can be redirected, a curse that can be broken. Every problem has a solution, and those solutions can be found as we seek the One who made us.

---

7 The Hebrew word *hhatah*

Recovery Involves an Exchange

Many of us have received a coupon in the mail for a free sandwich. What was in it for the vendor? New customers? Increased sales? When you handed the coupon to the cashier, they gave you the sandwich. In other words, when we *redeemed* the coupon, we got what was written on the coupon. An exchange happened.

Redeeming humankind from the power of sin was the *unified* desire of the Creator God—Father, Son, and Spirit. What was in it for God, the vendor in this example? A renewed relationship with humanity and the restored purpose of humankind and earth.

Since every coupon represents the price of the item being offered, we need to understand what the cost of sin is to God. If we go back to basic multiplication, we see that wages (cost) multiplied by sin (missing the bulls-eye) equals death.[8] There is a cost whenever we miss the bulls-eye of God's ideal.

A legal aspect exists in this exchange as well. Because we all sin, we are lawbreakers. We follow in the steps of Adam and Eve by allowing our physical senses to trump God's instructions. We both rely on our reasoning and listen to the serpent's[9] suggestions, ignoring the fact that our vantage point as created beings is limited. We are indicted by perfect justice, imprisoned by sin, and given the death penalty. How do we get out of jail? Can we be released through good behavior?

---

8 Romans 6:23 For the wages of sin is death, but the gift of God is eternal life in Christ Jesus our Lord.

9 Genesis 3:1 Now the serpent was more cunning than any beast of the field which the LORD God had made. And he said to the woman, "Has God indeed said, 'You shall not eat of every tree of the garden'?"

Looking at how the Creator has introduced himself to humanity helps us comprehend the significance of the solution. Generations after Adam and Eve, we meet Moses, an Egyptian prince who discovered that he was an Israelite. Therefore, he was raised to worship many gods. The Creator introduced Himself to Moses as I AM in Exodus 3:14. Hearing this name helped Moses understand that the entity speaking to him was self-sustaining, enduring, present, and the origin of power. He stands alone as divine. The English translation of "I AM" is Lord or God. The book of Revelation describes how God presented Himself to John, who was an original disciple of Christ. John heard these words: "I am the Alpha and the Omega, the First and the Last, the Beginning and the End." Again, we find the Creator self-defining as preeminent—that is, as the Originator.

As the originator of everything in existence, God is chief authority and judge. To be just and satisfy the legal require-ment—God had to make death a part of the solution. Good behavior wouldn't cut it. The penalty of sin—death had to be transferred somewhere else. In the early days, sin offerings were unblemished animals. A priest would put his hands on the animal, signifying that the people's sins were transferred to that animal. The animal was then killed. But the life of an ani-mal doesn't equal the life of a human being. How do we know this? Because only humans are made in the image of God. God determined that the only way to destroy the infection of sin for all time was for a human being to become the offering. Life for life.[10]

---

10 Genesis 9:5 Surely I will require your lifeblood; from every beast I will require it. And from every man, from every man's brother I will require the life of man.

The word *offering* means giving and then getting something in return. The Bible teaches that God came to earth as a human being so that He could be the *offering* for our sin. He was, in a manner of speaking, the "coupon" that was traded in on our behalf so that we could have something of great worth—life through a renewed relationship with the Life-Giver.

What was written on the coupon that He provided to us? The name *Jesus, the Christ.*

As Culture Changers, the person and life of Jesus present a problem. How can we assure someone that healing of spirit, soul, and body is possible if that person doesn't believe that Jesus was the offering—God in human flesh? There are so many people doing incredible work to bring healing around the world who don't worship Jesus as God—what do we say to them?

Finding out what many belief systems agree on is a good starting point.

One Truth or Many?

There are a vast number of faiths or spiritual belief systems. What they all have in common is worthwhile to remember:

- Evil
- Death (the end of our current physical reality)
- Concept of justice
- Concept of suffering
- Concept of good
- Desire to realign with a higher state of being

Making a case for one spiritual belief system over another legitimately puts millions of people on the defensive. Although for thousands of years, millions of people from every ethnicity have been convinced that Jesus was the divine offering for sin, non-Christians have a right to be dismissive, if not offended, at the statement that "Jesus Christ is the only way to eternal life."

The concept of eternal life refers to existing with the Creator in absolute shalom. Every belief system offers a way to eternal existence, but there is a difference between eternal existence and eternal life. At death, our physical bodies decompose, but our spirit/soul part exists *somewhere* and in some state. When Adam and Eve sinned, their physical bodies did not die; their spirits and souls became separated—disjointed from God. This separation is the state of darkness, chaos, confusion, lawlessness, and brokenness—the opposite of shalom. Peace, harmony, and wholeness cannot exist apart from God and His realm. In Greek, the word *life* is *zoe* and means present physical and future spiritual existence. Jesus calls Himself the *zoe* and describes Himself as the door. A door takes us from one room to another, from one condition to another state. Sin is the prison that none of us asked for, but our human bloodline gave us. But Jesus is the door to eternal life.

Lee Strobel has powerfully answered the questions that thousands ask about the relevancy of Jesus Christ in the face of other belief systems.

"It was the evidence from science and history that prompted me to abandon my atheism and become a Christian."[18]

In his book, *The Case for Christ,* Strobel shares with readers an interview he did with D.A. Carson, PH.D. Carson says,

> The overthrowing of slavery, then, is through the transformation of men and women by the gospel rather than through merely changing an economic system. We've all seen what can happen when you merely overthrow an economic system and impose a new order. The whole communist dream was to have a 'revolutionary man' followed by the 'new man.' Trouble is, they never found the 'new man.' They got rid of the oppressors of the peasants, but that didn't mean the peasants were suddenly free—they were just under a new regime of darkness. In the final analysis, if you want lasting change, you've got to transform the hearts of human beings. And that was Jesus' mission.[19]

While any person, regardless of worldview, can accept that the Bible and specifically Jesus Christ taught some profound universal lessons such as "love your enemies" or "a house divided against itself cannot stand"—real change comes when someone adheres to what the Bible teaches about Jesus, sin and the need for redemption. A person's core beliefs dramatically affect how they approach healing. Our beliefs, or worldviews, are shaped by what we've been taught and what we've "caught" from our families, our influencers, our textbooks, and even pop culture. Strobel concludes that only when we grasp and are living out the full picture of redemption can we bring individual triune healing, family repair, and community transformation.

Before they ate the fruit, Adam and Eve were meant to live forever; they dwelled in a land where there was no death. Through the family line of Abraham, God established a system for removing sin; the lives of unblemished lambs were taken as a blood sacrifice. Blood was required because, as Leviticus 17:11 says, the life of the flesh is in the blood. However, this was an imperfect system. As stated previously, the life of an animal is not equivalent to the life of a human being, and only sinless blood can satisfy the cost. Since all humanity was infected, God articulated His love and redemption power by taking on human flesh. Jesus Christ is the fullness of the triune God in bodily form.[11] The key that separates biblical salvation from any other type is that good behavior or *works*, does not return us to shalom. Redemption is received by faith, not earned through actions or deeds.

A Closer Look at Jesus Christ

Jesus or *Yehoshua* in the Hebrew is most easily translated as God saves. The Greek word Christos is actually a title that means anointed one from God.

...the Holy Spirit descended on Him in bodily form like a dove, and a voice came from heaven, "You are My Son, My Beloved, in You I am well-pleased and delighted!" (Luke 3:22 AMP)

For in Him all the fullness of Deity (the Godhead) dwells in bodily form [completely expressing the divine essence of God]. (Colossians 2:9 AMP)

The triune existence of God can be challenging to understand—Father, Son, Spirit. The first chapter of Genesis gives

---

11 Col. 2:9 For in Him all the fullness of Deity dwells in bodily form.

us a glimpse of the unity and function of the Godhead in Creation.

The command, "Let" released power to manifest and form all that was and is intended. This pronouncement conveys authority—the release of unified intent. John 1 calls Jesus Christ "the Word of God." The Word—the communicating instrument of the Godhead—spoke the command. The Spirit of God[12] is the breath or life force of the Godhead.

Jesus was born a man—He was human[13]—but He didn't have the infection of sin. How is this possible? Sin didn't transfer to His blood because He didn't have a human father. A mother's ovum has no blood, but sperm carries blood, from which sin is passed down from generation to generation. So as the New Testament Gospels record, Jesus was born from the egg of Mary and the sperm (or seed) of God's power (Matt. 1:18–25).

Sin cannot remove sin. So the sin of humanity was transferred to Jesus, who had no sin. He presented Himself in exchange for our freedom. When Jesus was dying on the cross, He called out to *Abba*, the Aramaic word for the male parent in the most personal, intimate sense. Then, the Word spoke, "It is finished," as the offering work of the Godhead was complete. To satisfy the requirement of sin, a human being needed to die, because death is the ultimate penalty. Redemption is the legal exchange—sin for righteousness.

---

12 *Ruach Elohim*, Hebrew

13 John 1:14 And the Word became flesh, and dwelt among us, and we saw His glory, glory as of the only begotten from the Father, full of grace and truth.

In beautiful detail, the Amplified version of Colossians 1 describes Jesus Christ as God in human form. The following passage displays the significance of Christ and what He's done for humanity:

He is the exact living image [the essential manifestation] of the unseen God [the visible representation of the invisible], the firstborn [the preeminent one, the sovereign, and the originator] of all creation. For by Him all things were created in heaven and on earth, [things] visible and invisible, whether thrones or dominions or rulers or authorities; all things were created and exist through Him [that is, by His activity] and for Him. And He Himself existed and is before all things, and in Him all things hold together. [His is the controlling, cohesive force of the universe.]He is also the head [the life-source and leader] of the body, the church; and He is the beginning, the firstborn from the dead, so that He Himself will occupy the first place [He will stand supreme and be preeminent] in everything. For it pleased the Father for all the fullness [of deity—the sum total of His essence, all His perfection, powers, and attributes] to dwell [permanently] in Him (the Son), and through [the intervention of] the Son to reconcile all things to Himself, making peace [with believers] through the blood of His cross; through Him, [I say,] whether things on earth or things in heaven. And although you were at one time estranged and alienated and hostile-minded [toward Him], participating in evil things, yet Christ has now reconciled you [to God] in His]physical body through death, in order to present you before the Father holy and blameless and beyond reproach— [and He will do this].

We have to agree and redeem this "coupon" that He has handed to us. The Bible teaches that the exchange comes through the following process:

1) We acknowledge that we are infected with sin.

2) We acknowledge that Jesus Christ is the Word of God[14] and became human to provide the way for us to be free from sin.

3) We acknowledge that the cross is the transaction point. The penalty of death happened on the cross.

4) Legally, death could not hold him, so on the 3rd day, He rose from the dead and later ascended to the Father. All things exist through Him and for Him.

When we verbally acknowledge the significance of Jesus' death, burial, and resurrection, our infection is removed. The reward we receive is a renewed relationship with God as our Abba, release from the power of sin, and the ability to discover His original intent for our lives. This miraculous, unseen exchange is the bedrock of triune healing.

> *Wash me thoroughly from my iniquity*
> *And cleanse me from my sin.*
> *For I know my transgressions,*
> *And my sin is ever before me.*
> *Against You, You only, I have sinned*
> *And done what is evil in Your sight,*

---

14 John 1:1 In the beginning was the Word, and the Word was with God, and the Word was God.

So that You are justified when You speak
And blameless when You judge.
Behold, I was brought forth in iniquity,
And in sin my mother conceived me.
Behold, You desire truth in the innermost being,
And in the hidden part You will make me know wisdom.
Purify me with hyssop, and I shall be clean;
Wash me, and I shall be whiter than snow. (Psalm 51:2–7)

NOTES
18. Strobel, Lee. *The Case for Christ: A Journalist's Personal Investigation of the Evidence for Jesus.* Grand Rapids, MI: Zondervan, 1998.

19. Ibid.,

CHAPTER ELEVEN

Our Own Triune Health

The Overlap of Spirit, Soul, and Body

*For the word of God is living and active and full of power
[making it operative, energizing, and effective]. It is sharper
than any two-edged sword, penetrating as far as the division of
the soul and spirit [the completeness of a person], and of both
joints and marrow [the deepest parts of our nature], exposing
and judging the very thoughts and intentions of the heart.*
(HEBREWS 4:12 AMPLIFIED BIBLE)

Sociologists and theologians alike understand that humans
are triune beings. Their understanding is supported by brain
researchers, psychologists, and behavioral scientists who the-
orize that there are three levels of mental processes. While
some of these theories provide substance for ongoing debate
(like those of Sigmund Freud and American neuroscientist
Paul MacLean), most people accept the conscious, subcon-

scious, and unconscious states of being. These states are parts of the human soul, where our will, emotions, and thoughts reside.[15]

Transforming the Spirit and Soul

The idea of understanding *who* we are and *how* we are has fascinated scientists and theologians for centuries. From the Greek schools of thought by Plato and Socrates to contemporary views expressed through faith, science, or metaphysics, human beings have attempted to understand how we are "soft-wired" to function. Earlier, the topic of sin and redemption was presented. Now, let's go a step deeper into how the spirit, soul, and body must work together to bring wholeness.

Our brain is the hardware that runs almost everything about us. It interfaces with our software—our soul and spirit in ways we are just beginning to understand. What is most important to realize is that every part of our composition interacts with and is closely linked to all the others. Christian redemption unbinds our spirits from the power of sin. However, our minds and physical bodies remain unchanged and can serve "the law of sin" if we allow them to do so.

Paul, born a Roman Jew, had experienced a remarkable and miraculous transformation in his *thinking* and *behavior*. He became a follower of Jesus after realizing the truthfulness of Christian testimony through a supernatural experience.

---

15 The back of the book will include a list of books I recommend for anyone who wants to do more research on these topics. I believe it is vital for anyone who has the heart of a Culture Changer to widen their base of knowledge and understanding. In many ways, my book makes just a minor dent in these topics.

As a result, he stopped murdering Christians. In Romans 7, he teaches that believers have a re-born spirit that is cleansed from sin, but they can still do evil things, and this reality vexes him.

> I find then a law, that evil is present with me, the one who wills to do good. For I delight in the law of God according to the inward man. But I see another law in my members, warring against the law of my mind, and bringing me into captivity to the law of sin which is in my members. O wretched man that I am! Who will deliver me from this body of death? I thank God—through Jesus Christ our Lord! So then, with the mind I myself serve the law of God, but with the flesh the law of sin.[16]

Romans 12:1 teaches us how to change our mindset to prefer good over evil. "Do not be conformed to this world, but be transformed by the renewing of your mind, so that you may prove what the will of God is, that which is good and acceptable and perfect." This *renewing* process is the science of neuropathways and neuroplasticity, as discussed in Chapter Seven.

Paul's charge is for Christians to be proactive when it comes to obtaining their triune health. The regular work of mind renewal and emotional self-evaluation is needed. Redemption has already removed the infection, but the relational journey with God empowers believers to align their minds and emotions with *shalom*.

---

16 Romans 7:21–25

Divine Alignment

We are born with an unbridled bent toward sin. As we mature, we recognize that we are *the created,* not *the Creator,* which means we can't know what is best. Therefore, submission to God is necessary. Once we are spiritually realigned with Him, God can walk alongside us, and we begin to live the life we were *created for.* This journey is based on a relationship. As we learn how to engage with Him, we exchange human ways of thinking for divine, selfishness for servanthood, and human weakness for divine enablement.

Aligning the human spirit and soul with God is the key to wholeness. *This* is the ultimate "centering," a phrase that some holistic practitioners use when teaching people how to ground themselves and find peace. God can remove sin's infection and mold us into the design He envisioned; however, this can occur only with those of us who have chosen to acknowledge Him, which is a decision of the soul.

The fact that our inner world—soul and spirit—are invisible to our physical eyes can be problematic and lead to skepticism when it comes to how soul healing occurs. The mind—or as I previously referred to it, the software of the brain—is sometimes used interchangeably with the word "spirit," which can cause some confusion. But here is the crux of the matter: each part of us needs to be *readjusted* to promote a constructive and healthy future.

The Soul and Behavior

Since lasting community transformation begins through one-on-one relationships, it is vital for Culture Changers to understand what makes people tick. Our thoughts, good and bad, affect our emotions, which in turn can positively or negatively affect our bodies. Rules, laws, or consequences deter unacceptable behavior but do not heal the soul. The story of Tommie Scott, former leader of the LA gang the Crips, is an example of how this works. Scott grew up in an environment that nurtured criminal activity as a way of life. Coupled with the mental and emotional trauma of living with an abusive father, he turned to drugs and crime. His turnaround, which occurred when he was in prison, clearly reveals how redemption and emotional healing can completely transform a person's circle of influence.

> Before being saved, I was suicidal and depressed. I destroyed lives by making others join gangs, sell drugs, and take part in robberies and violence. I couldn't provide for my family; I couldn't get a job because of my record and prison sentences. I felt low, worthless, and unloved. I hated myself...God started using me daily. I would pray for at least one soul to witness to each day. One day I caught the wrong bus and met a man who was going home to commit suicide because his wife had passed away. He had seven bottles of vodka in a bag, so I sparked a talk with him and found out about his wife and unbelief. After sharing with him, we two grown men on the bus went from crying to laughing in front of many people...God supernaturally transformed me.[20]

Not everyone's turnaround will be so dramatic that they're immediately able to minister to others. What brought about Scott's epiphany was the story of Paul, who, like himself, was a murderer. In a sense, Paul's testimony related to Scott so much that he didn't need a long process with someone walking alongside him to make him aware of his need to be made whole. Scott had reached his rock bottom. His story underscores that spiritual regeneration, according to the Christian faith, can bring forth transformation in a person's soul. Once his soul began to heal, Scott became a Culture Changer.

The Impact of Senses on Memory

Epigenetic memory works in tandem with our unique individual stories. We experience life through our senses, which leaves an impression on our brains and forms memories. We could say that these new memories go into the same "room" as our inherited memories.

The Bible reveals that what we speak, what we see, and what we hear affects the unseen parts of us.

Eyes that focus on what is beautiful bring joy to the heart, and hearing a good report refreshes and strengthen the inner being.
(Proverbs 15:11 TPT)

Let's take a closer look at the power of sight.

Vision

We experience vision on two planes: our imagination and the world around us. Our brains record *every* image, whether real or imagined. In this way, the inner world of someone who grows up in a neighborhood of manicured lawns is different than that of a person who grows up in a house with bars on the windows.

Visual stimulation is the crux of television, movie, and computer graphics. The downside is that in our brokenness, visual stimulation can also become a source of addiction and seduction. Pornography, for instance, is not just an individual issue; it can be an inherited addiction.

Similarly, as a nation enamored with pop culture, materialism, and general prosperity, we are often propelled to want the latest fan gear, smartphone, or house upgrades. The desire for beautiful things is not sinful—the problem comes when we elevate or prioritize our wants or specifically *what we see* above spiritual health and emotional maturity.

Mother Theresa lived among the poor, but she intentionally focused on the beauty of serving. She had the ability not to let the conditions around her dictate her emotional well-being. Our focus—our perspective of any given situation can strongly impact how we live.

I attended elementary school with a lot of wealthy kids. My middle-class neighborhood was on the edge of Shaker Heights, Ohio, and contained four-bedroom homes and nicely maintained yards. I can still remember my reaction when I first saw the large, stately mansions of my friends. It startled me, and I began to develop a sense of mediocrity because what I saw formed an impression in my brain. I was just a child and didn't have the tools to process my perceptions well. As a result, I always felt unsatisfied, even though I've lived in average suburban houses. I struggled with this perception even into my married years. Whenever I saw a house that was bigger and better than mine, I could feel a yearning deep inside.

So I did for myself what I help other people do—discover the thoughts, memories, and reasonings that evoked my emotional response. That is one way we can heal the soul. Through this process, I realized that my adult dissatisfaction was tied to my childhood feeling of mediocrity—feeling like I didn't measure up to the rich. Deep inside, I believed that until I had a beautiful mansion, I had not accomplished anything. Here's the lesson—what we *see* makes an impression not only on our brains but also on our souls.

Hearing and Speaking

For the overflow of what has been stored in your heart will be seen by your fruit and will be heard in your words. (Luke 6:45b TPT)

What we hear also has the power to determine our emotional wellbeing. Words carry weight. Spoken words and social media posts, no matter how casual, can hit a target in someone else's soul. Bullying has become an epidemic because every word carries power—the DNA of a seed that plants itself in the human soul and releases definition. We can reinforce generational iniquity through the words we speak if we say things like, "You have your great-aunt's temper," and not realize what we are doing.

Matthew 12:34 says, "Out of the abundance of the heart the mouth speaks." If we think of our hearts as mansions with many rooms that correspond to memories, specific ages, and life experiences, then we inevitably voice what occupies those rooms.

Consider a married couple. Let's say Todd's mother was a worrywart, and when he was a child, her vocalizing used to make him feel insecure. Now, whenever Todd's wife says something that implies worry, he responds out of that memory or "room" in his heart. His angry reactions reveal his childhood insecurity. Not only do they affect his marriage, but they also go on to influence the next generation because Todd's children are impacted every time he yells at their mother. Though he doesn't intend this outcome, his tongue is setting "on fire the course"[17] of his life and his kids' lives. He needs to realize and process the root of his anger and come to understand how these outbursts are tied to his childhood insecurity brought about through his mother's worry.

The Physical Body

The health of our physical bodies is connected to the state of our spirits and souls. This interconnectedness goes two ways. The condition of our bodies and what we do with them can affect our emotional wellbeing. Likewise, spiritual, mental, and emotional stress can have adverse effects on the body.

Many people, religious or secular-minded, view the *goodness* of the physical body differently. But no matter what we believe, our bodies can be a stumbling block to overall wellness if biological needs preoccupy our focus. If we spend all of our time focused on our physical needs, we can end up embracing practices and lifestyles that lead away from emotional and mental health.

To eliminate an unhealthy focus, many people of various religious faiths practice a type of fasting (abstinence, typically from food) or deny the physical body as an act of producing self-control and submission. Evangelical Christians and Muslims use fasting as both a practical and symbolic way of obtaining a posture of surrender and allowing extra time for prayer and study. Biblical fasting is a private decision[21] and can be done in a variety of ways, some of which

---

17 James 3:6 And the tongue is a fire, a world of iniquity. The tongue is so set among our members that it defiles the whole body, and sets on fire the course of nature; and it is set on fire by hell.

cause documented health benefits to the physical body such as detoxification. Some religious people believe the physical body is inherently evil; they believe that willful resistance to natural desires or physical exertion of self-denial will produce inward purity.

Self-flagellation, a thirteenth-century Roman Catholic practice, also known as mortification of the flesh, is on one side of the spectrum. The idea is that inflicting physical pain on the body brings identification with the death of Christ. Even some Shia Islam followers practice a form of flagellation during the festival of Ashura, which includes continually hitting themselves with various instruments even after blood appears.[22] The contrast of self-flagellation is the practice of hedonism, which is the idea that physical pleasure should not be ignored or denied. One undercurrent of this view is that fulfillment comes not from the inside out—spirit and soul to the body—but from the outside in, where physical satisfaction determines inner contentment. Lastly, *occultism* is an umbrella term for a vast array of mystical beliefs. These practices use self-harm, physical torture, and ritualistic sexual activity to promote enlightenment, spiritual growth, and surrender to the object of worship.

Any good practice or discipline can become an unhealthy ritual if done with the wrong motivation. A whole, healthy person understands they have the freedom[18] to refrain from a particular practice or ritual and know that God still accepts them. When they feel obligated to do something or continue

---

18 2 Corinthians 3:17 Now the Lord is the Spirit, and where the Spirit of the Lord is, there is liberty

a practice out of fear, shame, or worry, this is a sign that they have become bound to something in an unhealthy way. We need to help people understand the emotional, psychological, and spiritual consequences of any practices done because of outside pressure.

Followers of Jesus Christ understand that their physical bodies belong to Him[19], and He wants the human body taken care of in ways that align with His intent for health and vitality. While our biology dictates the meeting of needs—hunger, sexual desire, and sleep—the refusal of these things can cause physical harm when done in the extreme or in a way that does not consider emotional health. The link between biological needs and emotional health is clear. A lack of food and sleep causes irritability and difficulty with mental focus, plus many other side effects. The meeting of sexual desire without restraint and protection can lead to venereal disease and unwanted pregnancies. Sexual promiscuity and addiction can result in financial problems, broken homes, and relationship issues.

At the same time, viewing sexual desire as "evil" can produce guilt for any human being because sexual desire is mostly biological. Limiting marital sexual intimacy can stir negative emotions like bitterness and mistrust, and it can potentially even lead to infidelity. The Bible wisely urges husbands and wives to abstain from sexual intimacy only for a limited

---

19 1 Corinthians 6:19 Do you not know that your bodies are temples
of the Holy Spirit, who is in you, whom you have received
from God? You are not your own.

time.[20] Marriage brings a connection that ties the needs of the physical body to the health of the soul.

The Bible equates sexual union with marriage, a spiritual *covenant*. This mysterious binding of two individuals that is divinely endorsed affects the spirit and soul parts of each person. The recent endorsement of sexual freedom outside of marriage does not consider the *spiritual binding* of the participants. Most people just focus on the physical gratification and emotional fulfillment that occurs. However, triune health involves proper physical, emotional, *and* spiritual alignment with God's purposes.

As Culture Changers, we can empower people to acknowledge their emotional and physical needs and help them find healthy, constructive ways to meet some of those needs. Organizations, clinics, and ministries are great places to find professional guidance. Since some of these may focus on only one aspect of our triune makeup, getting input and assistance from a variety of resources is best. As we help people find these resources, we should remind them that unless it is aligned perfectly with the Creator's intent, every lens is skewed. Syncretism, the practice of combining various religious doctrine and spiritual beliefs, is common and unwise. People need to know *who* they are receiving from and remember that it is their responsibility to judge whether advice leads them to triune health or away from it. Counselors and healing

---

20 1 Corinthians 7:5 Stop depriving one another, except by agreement for a time, so that you may devote yourselves to prayer, and come together again so that Satan will not tempt you because of your lack of self-control,

practitioners can offer sound advice but also incorporate ideas that are not aligned with God's design and intent for humanity.

It is fascinating to consider human design—that we are beings created with material and immaterial parts that interface with one another. The more we grasp how the spirit, soul, and physical body work together, the better we can impart this information to others. In the next chapter, we will examine external forces that can help or hinder a person's journey toward wholeness.

NOTES
20. Carey Lodge Mon. "From Hit Man to Evangelist: How God Transformed a Notorious LA Gang Member." *Christian News on Christian Today*, www.christiantoday.com/article/from-hit-man-to-evangelist-how-god-transformed-a-notorious-la-gang-member/35872.htm.

21. Chavda, Mahesh. *The Hidden Power of Prayer and Fasting.* 2007

22. Newman, Andrew J. "Āshūrā." *Encyclopædia Britannica*, Encyclopædia Britannica, Inc., 27 June 2019, www.britannica.com/topic/Ashura-Islamic-holy-day.

CHAPTER TWELVE

More Than Meets the Eye

Our lives are powerful testimonies for the people God brings to us. Because of our "story," we can nurture them through any chapter in their "story." Our journey with them will give them the strength, encouragement, and vision to trade destructive behaviors and ways of thinking for constructive behaviors and positive ways of thinking. That person, in turn, will become a testament, and their family and friends will see the difference and eventually be impacted.

Sometimes after we've walked alongside someone for a while, we realize that despite getting their practical and emotional needs met, life isn't getting better for them. In these moments, we need to consider other realities that may be hindering their freedom. There could be facts outside of our vision, such as the story contained in the person's DNA or the influence of the spiritual realm.

Understanding the biblical lens is essential, especially in light of the person of Jesus Christ, who came not only to redeem but also to "destroy the works of the devil" (1 John 3:8).

Do you believe in spiritual realities? That something you cannot see can still affect your body, soul, or spirit?

In many cases, the words *unseen* and *invisible* are interchangeable and often refer to a realm beyond what our five physical senses can pick up. When it comes to human biology, our ears don't hear frequencies that are, in fact, in the range of many animals. A dog, for instance, can hear high-pitched sounds our ears don't register. Our physical hearing is limited, and we're constantly surrounded by sounds that we know nothing about. My points is, some things have to be sensed by the spirit—an unseen part of us that is distinct from our souls, although the two overlap in their activity.

When it comes to the *purpose* of the human spirit, Christianity, Hinduism, and New Age/occult belief have some significant theological differences, but their similarities support a universal reality that transcends any specific religious faith. In short, all that is visible was and is impacted by what we cannot see, and certain things can be discovered only by the human spirit. Eastern religions, quantum physics, metaphysics, Judeo-Christianity, and even occult beliefs support that idea, but the language of each view is different. Also, there is a disagreement between them about how we should interact with the invisible realm, as well as the existence of other beings that operate within that realm. When considering the process by which a person obtains triune health, the unseen realm cannot be ignored.

How Science "Sees" the Spiritual Realm

All of the electromagnetic spectrum is part of God's glory.
From gravity waves to the speed of light...
DAVID VAN KOEVERING

We've taken a look at how the Bible and natural science is compatible when it comes to our internal world of DNA and iniquity. Now we will look at how quantum science validates an external realm that we cannot see, but one that affects us daily.

Quantum physicist and inventor David Van Koevering found evidence that matter changes form when it "senses" a human being observing it. Because of his scientific discoveries and his musical background, he was able to use the language of science to explain Scriptures such as Colossians 1:16: "For by Him all things were created, both in the heavens and on earth, visible and invisible." The verse says that everything we see was made from things we can't see. For the physicist or chemist, this is accurate—matter is too small to see with our physical eyes. Brittanica defines quantum physics this way:

The behaviour of matter and radiation on the atomic scale often seems peculiar, and the consequences of quantum theory are accordingly difficult to understand and to believe. Its concepts frequently conflict with common-sense notions derived from observations of the everyday world. There is no reason, however, why the behaviour of the atomic world should conform to that of the familiar, large-scale world. It is important to realize that quantum mechanics is a branch of physics and that the business of physics is to describe and account for the way the world—on both the large and

139

the small scale—actually is and not how one imagines it or would like it to be.[23]

The invisible realm is a somewhat common theme in the Bible. Here is another reference:

Now faith is the assurance (certainty) of things hoped for, the conviction of things not seen—By faith we understand that the worlds were prepared by the word of God, so that what is seen was not made out of things which are visible.[21]

Key points in these verses can help us understand why Van Koevering and scientists like Albert Einstein and Max Planck, were convinced that quantum physics could prove certain spiritual realities.

In addition to mentioning the unseen or invisible world, the Scriptures also reference Jesus Christ as the Word of God or divine articulator of what we see and what we don't see. Some Christians say that what God the Father purposes, Jesus speaks forth, and the Spirit of God performs.

Energy does not create itself; it must have a source or energizer...Genesis has provided reasonable evidence to conclude that God not only created matter but also started the vibrations at the center of it...the book of Colossians includes the invisible realm in its description of creation.[24]

The biology of our physical body has limitations; therefore, it is logical to think that spiritual realities are best discerned through our *spirit*.

---

21 Hebrews 11: 1,3

The authors of *The Physics of Heaven* write:

> As human beings, we are only able to see about 3 percent of the entire light vibratory spectrum (we call it visible light) and probably only able to hear that much of the sound vibratory spectrum. This means there is a whole realm of energy and vibration we can't see with our eyes or hear with our ears. Could it be that God has given us other ways to sense the unseen and unheard? [25]

Considering that the Bible says human beings have "light," which we know is based on energy, it is reasonable that created beings that occupy the unseen realm also have what can be identified as energy—the good-willed ones carry "good" energy, and the evil-intentioned ones emitting negative energy. This rough characterization is supported by the Bible's identification of angels and evil spirits. The Bible lists various types or levels of malevolent entities in Ephesians 6:12, a verse which discusses the intent to thwart human affairs: "For we do not wrestle against flesh and blood, but against principalities, against powers, against the rulers of the darkness of this age, against spiritual hosts of wickedness in the heavenly places."

How do all of these ideas affect Culture Changers?

We can communicate universal similarities to help people of different faiths consider how they can obtain triune health. When we're looking for remedies for the dilemma of human brokenness, the unseen realm needs to be considered. If it is true that malevolent beings are trying to impede our lives, then we need to learn how to prohibit their ability to hinder us! Said another way, if biological energy can be negative or positive, human beings need to learn how to *repel* destructive energies.

For Culture Changers, the spirit realm needs to be part of the equation as we seek to bring wholeness to individuals. If an unseen world of evil exists, it is crucial to decide whether our assignment is to fight against it or just survive in spite of it. As we journey into wholeness, how do we equip ourselves to repel evil and resist its influence? How would we help others do the same? Andrew Murray, a well-known South African pastor of the nineteen century, wrote:

> ...the believer yields himself to the leading of the Holy Spirit, without claiming to have it first made clear to the intellect what He is to do, but consenting to let Him do His work in the soul, and afterward to know what He has wrought there. Faith trusts the working of the Spirit unseen in the deep recesses of the inner life. And so the word of Christ and the gift of the Spirit are to the believer sufficient guarantee that he will be taught of the Spirit to abide in Christ. By faith he rejoices in what he does not see or feel: he knows and is confident that the blessed Spirit within is doing His work silently but surely, guiding him into the life of full abiding and unbroken communion. The Holy Spirit is the Spirit of life in Christ Jesus; it is His work, not only to breathe, but ever to foster and strengthen, and so to perfect the new life within. And just in proportion as the believer yields himself in simple trust to the unseen, but most certain law of the Spirit of life working within him, his faith will pass into knowledge.[26]

Biblical faith *requires* belief in an unseen realm. That there is *more* to life than what we see—invisible activity behind the scenes of every crime, protest, and occurrence of injustice. Christians believe that God not only directs benevolent armies of angels to help people but also that He endows believers with the ability to repel the influence of evil. If evil is more than an idea but actual beings, with energy void of goodness and purity, then we need to identify them correctly so that we can oppose them.

What's Real and What's Just "Imagination"?

We do not need more intellectual power, we need more spiritual power. We do not need more of the things that are seen, we need more of the things that are unseen.
CALVIN COOLIDGE

Most of us are familiar with at least a few of the monsters, giants, and devils found in art and myths. As children, we probably watched cartoons, where the devil with horns and a pitchfork tried to push the main character to do something we all knew was wrong.

Humanity has always been interested in characterizing or trying to depict what evil looks like. Is the Bible's explanation of evil beings correct? Do they actually exist? More than just the Judeo-Christian world would say yes. Though the concept of an unseen realm is irrelevant to people whose worldview is based on tangible evidence and proof, people all around the world are convinced of the reality of unseen living entities, both benevolent and evil. Some of these entities are even worshipped by various people groups; others are viewed as agents of God's divine will or the opponents of His will.

If we accept the idea of created life forms existing in an unseen realm or dimension, we can take the next *logical* step and start to understand how their existence intersects with the lives and affairs of human beings, communities, and systems.

The Enemy Behind the Scenes

When I was a kid, the idea of witchcraft and the occult felt dangerous and strange, so I stayed away from library books with mystical and scary themes. Although I went to church, my pastors never taught about the spiritual war in the Bible, so I believed that anything scary was a product of people's imagination. This belief caused me to assume the devil wasn't actually real. Without proper training, how could I have believed anything different?

As a young adult, I began to read my Bible and found confirmation of a spiritual realm that is as real as the visible world. Interesting verses like Colossians 1:16 are peppered throughout the New Testament: "For by Him all things were created that are in heaven and that are on earth, visible and invisible." As I continued forward in my faith journey, I discovered that we have a responsibility as it relates to invisible things.

The Bible teaches that individuals are influenced and impacted by unseen forces of evil that are purposeful in their mission (Ephesians 6:12–18). A hierarchy of evil entities attempts to steal, kill, and destroy God's intent for all created order. For our purposes, this means that nothing happens "by chance." Whenever we're talking about gun violence, prejudice, or any other social pain, there is an unseen cause behind it. Sin is but one cause; another is found in the invisible realm.

When it comes to helping people find healing,[22] we have to acknowledge that the Creator, as healer and redeemer, cannot cause or approve of the mission of this unseen realm of

---

22 A list of resources that delve into this topic are listed in the back of this book.

evil. While there are spiritual and natural laws, of which God as a Just Lawgiver binds Himself to, the Bible discloses that He gave humanity authority in the earth. He appointed us as stewards who have a choice to bring wholeness to the world or perpetuate brokenness by aligning ourselves with the mission of evil entities.

Here's the overarching story of Scripture:

- Lucifer, a created being, sinned against JHVH (the Hebrew word for God) and was dismissed, along with other created beings, from God's presence (Isaiah 14).

- God created man and woman with free will, provided them with all they needed, and gave one admonition: not to eat from a specific tree (Genesis 2).

- An evil entity, in a serpent's body, successfully tempted Adam and Eve to ignore God's warning.

- God put His redemption plan into action: to destroy the hold that evil had over humanity and to bring humanity back into His intended purpose.

Releasing humanity from the captivity of sin and demonic oppression involves salvation in Jesus Christ (spiritual redemption), renewing one's mind (soul restoration), and offering willful submission to God's design for our physical bodies (physical wellness). Finally, we are invited to partner with Him to bring light where there is darkness.

The one who practices sin is of the devil; for the devil has sinned from the beginning. The Son of God appeared for this purpose, to destroy the works of the devil. (1 John 3:8)

When we partner with this divine mission as Culture Changers, we help individuals recognize how unseen evil is active in their lives, how it has potentially affected their family lines, and how it continues to keep communities in disrepair. We then can help them unveil the darkness, break the cycles, and release the light of a benevolent God.

NOTES
23. Squires, Gordon Leslie. "Quantum Mechanics." *Encyclopædia Britannica,* Encyclopædia Britannica, Inc., 3 Aug. 2018, www.britannica.com/science/quantum-mechanics-physics.

24. From chapter excerpt of Dan McCollam's manuscript God Vibrations *The Physics of Heaven* by Judy Franklin and Ellyn Davis, p. 61

25. Franklin, Judy and Davis, Ellyn. *The Physics of Heaven*, p. 61

26. Murray, Andrew. *With Christ in the School of Prayer: Thoughts on Our Training for the Ministry of Intercession.* New York: A.D.F. Randolph, 1885.

CHAPTER THIRTEEN

God's Hand Moves When We Engage Him

Vertical first, horizontal second. This is how Culture Changers describe their lifestyle. Moment to moment engagement with our Creator revitalizes us when we are weak, teaches us when we do not understand, and reminds us that we do not heal, *He* does. So human relationships prosper if we make God first in our lives. We are just the vessels for His life-giving nature and supernatural power. Bringing the needs of others to Him in prayer is a work of service and love. Therefore, prayer must be the altar on which we leave the pain of others as well as our own pain.

Prayer is encountering God through verbal and non-verbal engagement. Almost daily, I go outside to my garden and sit. Getting away from manmade noise and the pace of family life helps me align my human spirit with the Spirit of God through prayer and contemplation. *Have I been too me-fo-*

cused and distracted by to-dos and possessions? These are questions that I ask as I re-center myself with God.

One afternoon, the needs of a friend were heavy on my heart. Before I spouted off all my questions and complaints, I recited various scriptures. Verses where God reveals who He is and what He is like. My encounter with God in those minutes involved letting His Word remind me of things that the urgency of her need had caused me to forget. His faithfulness. His mercy. Prayer is a wonderful interchange where our innermost thoughts are expressed, and He brings direction and comfort through His Word.

The foundation of prayer is faith. We are praying to a God we cannot see and asking Him to bring an answer for something we *can* see. While the answer may not come the moment we say, "Lord, help me," we can know that help is on the way through the power of His Spirit, His angels, and the ordained steps of others.

Engaging God involves trust and belief. We have to believe God is good and desires good for all people, even those we might label "evil." He doesn't bless their evil intentions and works, but He wants to endow them with the ability to know right from wrong and light from darkness. He ultimately wants every human being on a trajectory that will bring life to them and those around them. That is why Jesus told His disciples to bless those who cursed them and to pray for those who spitefully used and persecute them[23].

---

23 Matthew 5:44

People pray in different ways. Some prefer written prayers that can be personalized; prayer formats can be helpful at times to keep people focused. Many use the Lord's Prayer found in Matthew 6 as an outline or structure they can customize. As a new mother, my prayers were often quick requests for help, called *petitions*. Through the years, I learned *intercession*, which is praying for others. Formal or informal, written or spontaneous, our communication with God affects the unseen parts of our souls as well as the spiritual realm. As we worship God with our spirits, surrender the disposition of our souls (mind, will, and emotions) and verbalize scriptural prayers, His power will bring healing in broken places.

Engaging God in prayer is not the only way He works in the unseen parts of our being. Practicing *gratitude*—thanking Him helps our attitude. Positivity is a stress reliever. When we intentionally lift our eyes from our wounds and look through the gospels, we are reminded that He embraced our wounds to heal our wounds.

As practical as moments of thanksgiving are, so are times of *lament*. A lament is the acknowledgment of grief, the exercise of letting legitimate emotions pour forth in the safety of God's unconditional acceptance. Many passages in the Psalms reveal David's times of lament. This Old Testament book gives us a practical picture of grieving, that is, putting our feelings down on paper, emoting through a song, or releasing sorrow through tears.

God Sees Buried Pain

Sometimes God initiates our healing in surprising ways. Dreams are one. Although not every dream is significant, God has the power to penetrate our subconscious as we sleep.

These types of divinely inspired dreams are often symbolic, but we can learn how to understand what God is saying through them.

One dream of mine went like this: I was in a check-in line with my family, including my mother. We had to swipe our credit cards to enter, and the cards had to be from a recognized bank. Everyone's card was accepted—except mine, so I smiled, told everyone I was okay, and would just wait for them outside. I sat by myself on a bench and pretended to be okay.

Then the dream changed. This time I was sitting on steps outside a house. Some activity was happening inside the house, and when I found out what was going on, rage filled me.

At that point in the dream, I woke up, and I could actually feel the intensity of the emotion in my body. Somewhat coherent, I prayed silently, "Lord, what is this, where is it from, and what can You do about it?" In my groggy state, I tried to define the emotions that I felt: being taken advantage of, disrespected and rejected by those who were supposed to love me, and the frustration of being ignored.

When I fell back to sleep, the dream continued. I saw Jesus standing next to me. He asked, "What do you want to do to all those people who hurt you?"

My answer was to imagine myself running into the house and beating them. I saw various people, some related to me and some in my lineage.

The next thing I remember from my dream was seeing a little girl, raw and unclothed, with Jesus sitting behind her. The girl was me. Here is that dream:

Jesus took all my inner turmoil—the rage, the hurt, the rejection, the disrespect, and frustration—and put it in a huge bag. It smoked with the heat of my emotions.

Jesus said to me, "These feelings are just."

I blinked at Him in astonishment, and He repeated, "These feelings are just."

Then He asked, "Can I take this bag and keep it?"

I wondered why He would do that, and He told me it was a big bag, and it would be better for him to deal with the injustices His way. He said they *would* be dealt with. I liked that answer and nodded, and then I watched Him place the large, hot bag of my emotions far away from where we were. I shivered because I was unclothed.

He took His robe and put it on me and said, "Wear this. It will help you." I asked Him why, and He replied that His robe was mercy, grace, and forgiveness, and it would help me. I told him that it felt uncomfortable. It was a little big for me and didn't fit well.

"You aren't used to it," He said but assured me I would grow into it. I nodded my consent and trust in Him. He didn't leave but stayed and hugged me from behind, with His arms around me.

The message of the dream satisfied a distant hurt that I had no idea I carried. My desire for justice was right, but Jesus can bring forth justice better than I can. Whatever pain I had carried, but forgotten, was lifted and taken away by the unseen hand of the Lord.

Dreams like this have only happened a few times in my life. Through them, I learned that God heals in creative ways.

An Easy Way to Serve Others

Therefore I exhort first of all that supplications, prayers, intercessions, and giving of thanks be made for all men, for kings

and all who are in authority, that we may lead a quiet
and peaceable life in all godliness and reverence. For this is
good and acceptable in the sight of God our Savior,
who desires all men to be saved and to come to the
knowledge of the truth. (1 Timothy 2:2–4)

A few books that teach about prayer are listed in the Recommended Resources section at the back of this book. These books have given me the insight and tools to pray in a way I know is useful. Not everyone may be a "prayer warrior" (a term that charismatic circles often use for people who dedicate much of their time to intercede for others), but everyone can pray.

As a person gains the courage to escape their places of bondage and be healed from emotional pain, they may reach an intersection where they need us, as Culture Changers, to pray for them. We need to be confident and comfortable with our ability to pray.

God made Himself the sin offering we needed. He did this through the Son, Jesus, whom the Spirit of God raised from death. Many pray "in Jesus' name" in recognition that His shed blood is our only access door or way to salvation, eternal life, and divine alignment.

However, those specific words—"in the name of Jesus"— shouldn't be treated like some kind of mantra. Since the essence of prayer is a relationship with God through Jesus Christ, we can personalize our prayers to echo our understanding of Jesus' centrality.

Pray for your family and friends. When you're trying to help someone, offer to pray for them and be sure to pray for *their* family members and friends as well. Keep in mind that

God will use their testimony to bring life to those around them.

Personally, I think simple prayers are best. It lets the person know that even when you aren't there to pray for them, they can simply say, "God, help me," and that is enough to activate the power of God into their life (Psalm 91:15).

Pray for your neighbors. Pray as you drive around your city. Pray without ceasing (1 Thessalonians 5:17).

Praying for Those of Different Beliefs

In times of need, few people turn down prayer, even if they have a different belief system than the person offering to pray.

If there is a different belief system, or perhaps none at all, respectfully ask them if you can pray the way you pray for yourself. If they're uncomfortable with this, respect their discomfort. At some point in your relationship with them, they may ask for your prayers. You can do so on your own or in their presence.

A Few Ways to Pray for Your Community

1) "God, I want to partner with You to rebuild ruined communities. Help me restore Your intent for families in communities where You send me to serve. Give me and others the wisdom, love, and power to repair breaches between people groups. I ask this remembering the authority that Jesus Christ has given me as His fellow worker."[24]

---

24 See Isaiah 58:12; 1 Corinthians 3:9.

2) "I agree with God's desire for the dysfunctional cycles in this family to end. Father, may Your Spirit guide the members of this family to do things differently. I declare that the desire of God in Malachi 4:6 will come to pass in this family, that the hearts of parents will turn favorably toward their children, and the hearts of the children will turn favorably to their parents. I proclaim this in the mighty name of Jesus Christ, my Lord, and Savior."

3) "Lord, help this person forgive _____. Holy Spirit, please comfort them and heal them from their pain. Thank You, God."[25]

4) "Father, continue to heal _____ in all areas of their life. Show them the rooms in their heart where emotional wounds, inherited dysfunction, and ungodly mindsets remain. Help them keep You as the number one priority in their life. May the God of hope fill them with all joy and peace in believing, so that they will abound in hope by the power of the Holy Spirit." [26]

4) "I announce that wickedness in this neighborhood must surrender to the authority and name of Jesus Christ, who wants hope, vitality, and healing here. I speak the words of God in Isaiah 58:12 that He will build the old waste places; He will raise up the foundations of many generations. God is the Repairer of the Breach and the

---

25 See Colossians 4:2.

26 See Romans 15:13.

Restorer of Streets so we can dwell in safety. In Jesus'
name. Amen."

4) "Help _____ acknowledge their anger in a healthy
way, without harming others or themselves. Jesus,
according to Ephesians 4:26, show _____ your will-
ingness to remove their anger and any related emotions
in order to bring them peace. Restore their souls. Give
them hope in You. Amen."[27]

4) "Lord, release Your angels to battle against the dark
entities of evil in my city, to protect Your people and
help them. Bring your light, vision, and understanding
to places of oppression and confusion. Help me pray for
my city regularly according to Ephesians 6:10–18. With
the authority of the name of Jesus, I pray. Amen."[28]

God is more than a purpose-driven King. He is a Creator
who loves to interact with His people in places of solitude and
the energy of high praise. He is a Shepherd who will tune our
ear to hear His voice and comfort us when we're hurting. Even
Jesus prays for us from heaven.[29] If we don't keep fellowship
with Him as our top priority, we will end up steering our lives
out of presumption instead of leaning in and following His
Word.

---

27 See Psalm 23:3; Lamentations 3:24.

28 See 2 Thessalonians 1:6–8; Daniel 6:22; Psalm 78:49, 91:11.

29 Hebrews 7:25 Therefore He is able also to save forever those who draw near
to God through Him, since He always lives to make intercession for them.

CHAPTER FOURTEEN

How You Can Begin

*You cannot hope to build a better world
without improving the individuals.*
MARIE CURIE

*"What can you do to promote world peace? Go home
and love your family." "Do not wait for leaders;
do it alone, person to person."*
MOTHER TERESA

The epiphany is my favorite part of any movie or book. This literary device describes the moment when a character's internal conflict begins to resolve due to a change of perspective or a life-changing decision. My own life had a few of these intersections—one happened at a Methodist camp when I was sixteen, another during the spring of my junior year in college. The choices I made at these points shifted me toward triune healing. My epiphanies brought about the divine assignments that I walked in over the next thirty years. As a teenager, I would never have guessed that I would ever home school or do various types of ministry for people of different backgrounds.

In the 1994 drama *Shawshank Redemption,* Red's patience and kindness enabled the main character, Andy, to confess the pain he wrestled with. Through friendship, each man experienced an epiphany that eventually helped them escape the trauma of victimhood. Maya Angelou's autobiography, *I Know Why the Caged Bird Sings,* made quite an impression on me as a pre-teen. The embarrassment she felt when she forgot her lines in front of a church audience resonated with me. I understood her feelings of inadequacy. Her unhealthy lifestyle as a teen finally brought Maya to a point where she decided to leave her metaphorical Egypt— enslavement to both a community and an identity that stifled her divine purpose. For many of us, the process of escaping our "Egypts" involves unexpected intersections where we decide to choose a new path. That choice to change is an epiphany that shifts the rest of our lives.

To help others choose to move out of brokenness, we need to remind ourselves of the difficulties of our own journey. At that moment—our epiphany—some of us felt like we woke up from an anesthetized state. The unseen parts of us began to stir; we became aware of what had been brewing under the surface of our lives. Suddenly we felt the shame we were embarrassed to face. Or the anger we'd managed to suppress all this time began to flare up. We were blinded to unresolved hurts or unmet desires, and we lived as icebergs, with most of our personhood buried under the ocean surface.

That is the condition of most of the people we will meet. So they will need our steady hands as they become aware of their own soul wounds. As people become self-aware, we can give them ideas on how to meet the distinct needs of their spirit, soul, and body in constructive ways.

Our Role in the Solution

The word *edify* means to build up. As Culture Changers, we are called to *build up* those whose lives intersect with ours for a few minutes or a lifetime. We bring change as we oppose the conditions and mindsets that diminish the quality of life for individuals, families, and communities. As part of building up people, we come alongside people to help them obtain vision for their lives because vision is the force that will carry them through tough situations. Constructive choices will keep them moving forward in their emotional health and mental wellbeing.

We must remain patient, optimistic, and respectful of others' individuality. Someone might refuse what we may offer, but they have the freedom to choose their path.

Ideally, some people will begin to view life through a biblical lens. The Bible is the vehicle through which the Creator chose to communicate His intents and design to humanity. This lens provides the courage necessary to conquer personal pain and daily hindrances. The view is grace-oriented and acknowledges divine assistance; it is not works-based, which relies on human striving. Through this lens, people can adopt a missional way of living that encourages them to go out and become Culture Changers too. That is one of the key points of healing—as we're healed, we naturally go out and begin to heal others, and that is what changes the world.

Discovering Current Assignments

You may have stumbled across this book by accident. Perhaps a friend suggested that you read it. Whatever the case, if you've gotten this far, the subject matter obviously intrigues you for a reason. For some, the reforming work of a Culture Changer calls to a deep place within—one that has been pushing them to pursue a life-giving cause that is greater than themselves.

Maybe you're going through a spiritual awakening or becoming emotionally healthy right now. At some point, you recognized that the trajectory of your life was leading down a path that wouldn't bring peace, joy, and safety for you or those around you, and so you made a decision—an epiphany occurred. Or perhaps the possibility of community transformation and family repair, although complicated, invigorates your hope to see a change in your lifetime or your children's lifetime.

Here are some personal action points:

Think about the hardships you've overcome. Name at least one thing that you learned about yourself through them. Note any people that came alongside you to help you. What did they do or say that helped bring you into a place of victory?

Get comfortable with your story. Own where you've been and what you learned. Don't stay ashamed, feel guilty, or embrace condemnation for what your life has looked like up until now. Your Creator gave Jesus Christ to pay the price of your sin. You can believe this and choose to make Him the main focus of every area of your life. Embracing the meaning of Jesus Christ's death on the cross and His resurrection makes a big difference in a person's heart—an eternal difference. As you welcome this new identity—being a child of God—your brokenness will no longer enslave or define you. Jesus makes all things new[30].

If you're already a believer, you know what I'm talking about. You've chosen to embrace a journey of continual mind renewal, which leads to abundant life. What you've overcome, the lions and bears you've defeated, give you the authority to speak with confidence to those you meet along the way. God will lead you to those who need you. You'll get to walk alongside them for long periods or perhaps just for a single moment as you go about your day. An inspired word spoken at the right time gives life, and you are now a life-giver.

Many people have a limited view of salvation and the idea of release from sin. "Just getting into heaven" is an unfortunate simplification of the Christian redemption story. God desires humankind to be a family of kingdom dwellers. Therefore, He intends not just to rescue an individual from brokenness—but to rescue families and entire communities and manifest Himself through them to all creation[31]. As that happens, social systems will be impacted because many of the people who control them will admit their brokenness and want to be made whole.

Those from among you shall build the old waste places;
You shall raise up the foundations of many generations;
And you shall be called the Repairer of the Breach,
The Restorer of Streets to Dwell In. (Isaiah 58:12)

---

30 2 Corinthians 5:17
31 Romans 8:9 The entire universe is standing on tiptoe, yearning to see the unveiling of God's glorious sons and daughters! (TPT)

With this in mind, here are a few ways you can step out and begin to change the course of your community. Let's begin by talking about your health because that is always the first step. Your choice for health means other people will naturally begin to grow in their health as well.

- Remember to maintain your mental, emotional, spiritual, and physical wellbeing. You can't help someone else if you're worn out.

- Stay thankful for your story. The journey you're on is a testimony for someone else. Be grateful for the lessons you're learning in your relationships and challenging seasons.

- Take time each day to connect with God. Quietness is rewarding. Enter into this space aware that the One who created you is waiting to nurture your spirit and soul.

- Stay humble. No human being ever "arrives" at the peak of perfection. We will never know it all or have all the answers.

- Think about where you are on your journey toward triune health. Find additional resources that will help you grow.[32]

- Make sure you're in relationships with people who can encourage you in this endeavor and give wise advice. Commit to being emotionally honest with these people.

- Get practical training in helping people through trauma through organizations like the Trauma Healing Institute.

---

32 Check the resource page at the back of this book.

Study online resources available through non-profits like Adult Children of Alcoholics. Buy or find resources that will give you training and in-depth study on the topics that particularly interest you in this book.

- When in a public place, put your phone away and engage someone next to you. Respect their boundaries, and stop if they show disinterest.

- Invite a few neighbors, friends, or coworkers to read and discuss this book with you for a couple of months. Even if people differ in perspectives, a shared vision for community transformation can be a flame that grows.

- Greet everyone you meet with a look in the eye and a smile. Say thank you to the cashier. Leave the garbage man or the postal worker a simple note saying, "Thank you," or "Have a nice day."

- Simple acts of kindness and spontaneous conversations can act as leaven in our world.

- Take a few moments and consider the following words. Many consider King Solomon (990–931 BC) to be the wisest man who ever lived, and he had much to say about good and evil:

When wisdom enters your heart,
And knowledge is pleasant to your soul,
Discretion will preserve you;
Understanding will keep you,
To deliver you from the way of evil,
From the man who speaks perverse things,
From those who leave the paths of uprightness
To walk in the ways of darkness;

Who rejoice in doing evil,
And delight in the perversity of the wicked;
Whose ways are crooked,
And who are devious in their paths. (Proverbs 2:10–15)

Decide to give God your daily plans. In the Old Testament, Moses knew he was carrying out God's strategy with Pharaoh, but he didn't rush ahead. He waited for instructions before every encounter with the Egyptian leader. Similarly, David understood his purpose as the king, but he had no idea how God would use people and situations to fulfill His overall purpose for Israel. The Psalms reveal that David's main agenda was to fellowship with God.

CHAPTER FIFTEEN

Impacting Your First Circles of Influence

Families are the building blocks of communities. The visible aspects of those communities—neighborhoods, schools, workplaces, and churches—often reflect the triune health of the families represented. But outward appearance can be deceptive. Just because a community or a family inside it *looks* healthy doesn't mean it is. Dysfunction often lies hidden behind a façade and a smile. When we recognize hindrances and weaknesses inside ourselves, we can take steps to bring change—and those steps can lead those around us to make the same changes.

For example, let's say a mother recognizes that she and her husband have unintentionally raised their two young teens to be frivolous in their spending and lazy when it comes to being helpful around the house. After the couple learns the value of emotional honesty, they engage their teens in a series of heart-to-heart conversations that convey deliberate changes they're going to make as parents and why. They apologize for their failure to model self-sacrifice and self-control when it came to spending. They also tell their kids that while they cannot demand that the teens *like* future decisions, as a family, they are going to implement some changes like attending a local church. Over time, as the parents work on changing their own habits and behaviors, the teenagers begin to accept their parents' decisions and new lifestyle.

After the nuclear family, we can influence our families of origin, depending on our degree of relationship with them. Many extended family systems are spread across the nation due to educational and job opportunities; some reach a place where they have to experience healthy separation from their relatives in order to grow and become whole themselves. When we carry a divine burden for our extended family members, prayer is a practical and powerful answer.

Changing a family culture requires a different approach depending on your role or position in the family. A parent of minors has more ability to change the culture of their family than a teen member of a family or an adult within the extended family system. Since individuals have free will, merely telling your family members, "You need to stop this unhealthy behavior," will not work. It doesn't matter what the unhealthy behavior is—enabling addictions, calling each other names, disrespecting elders, making fun of others, etc. Behaviors and mindsets are like deep trenches in the brains *and* the soul. Whenever we find something that we want to change in our family, we need to live out that change ourselves first. What you can do by yourself:

1. Identify the destructive tendency.

2. Get a picture of what the family could look like when operating in a different mode.

3. Begin to behave and speak differently.

4. Create a manner about you that directly opposes the dysfunction, but stay humble.

5. Pray regularly and serve your family members in practical ways.

The most natural family to shift is your own—your sons and daughters who are the next generation. This generation is a canvas with undefined lines, but God sees its best prospects and every good thing it might become.

Unconditional acceptance, a sense of value and belonging, emotional connection, and mutual forgiveness are just a few elements that develop in a healthy family environment.

Family Action Plan

1. Purposefully Encourage Each Other

Have times of encouragement for things like birthdays, New Year's Eve parties, and the anniversaries of both joyous and traumatic events, etc. Setting aside moments of remembrance for these painful occasions can be healing, especially when the tendency is to repress pain and short-circuit the grief cycle.

My family calls these events *times of prayer and prophetic blessing* because we pray about the Scriptures that will encourage the family member. In the New Testament, prophecy is meant to edify, encourage, and comfort[33], so during these times, we impart positive words that can bring emotional healing. These times restore purpose, vision, hope, and energy, and they are excellent relationship builders.

Young children can be incorporated into these times through the creative arts: writing a simple poem, drawing a picture, making up a song for the person, etc.

2. Find Opportunities to Serve Together

Serving can happen through church events or community programs. As a family, you could invite neighbors to a cookout, bake cookies for them on holidays, or ask how they are and how you can help.

Years ago, an elderly white man lived up our street. In the beginning, our interaction was usually just a wave as we drove by. Some winters, I'd see him shoveling his driveway after an occasional hard snowfall. Somewhere along the line, we decided to rush to shovel it before he did. He would open his front door and wave in gratitude. One day, I took him Christmas cookies. His son answered the door and told me our neighbor had died. I gave the cookies to his son and let him know what a friendly man his dad had been and gave him my condolences. He was so impacted that he ended up deciding to sell the house to one of our family friends. These were such small gestures—but even small things can make a big difference.

---

33 1 Cor. 14: 3 But when someone prophesies, he speaks to encourage people, to build them up, and to bring them comfort. (TPT)

3. Read Books Together

Find books about historical or contemporary people who made a difference, and as a family, learn from their lives. When possible, read books that show your kids how one life can make a difference in the context of history. Develop within them a sense of mission and purpose. Allow time for questions, answers, and insight. If the older kids don't want to "sit" and listen to a parent reading, you may want to take turns reading the same book.

When our older children were teens, my husband and I began passing along to them several books we'd read. Now that they are adults, they do the same for us.

4. Have a Text or Email Group

When one of us comes across an article, post, or podcast we like or find interesting, we text or email the link to others in our family. It keeps us learning and discovering together, and it also provides topics for discussion. It is fun sharing jokes and new music as well. Not only do I do this with my husband and adult children, but with my mother and siblings. Distance does not have to hinder connection.

5. Research Your Family Lineage

Share and record family stories that have been passed down through generations. This brings a sense of identity and belonging and allows for inherited giftings and skills to be discovered.

We were able to trace a few family lines back to enslaved ancestors and discover the families of slave owners who impregnated our slave ancestors. As we processed these findings, we were able to walk through deeper levels of forgiveness.

We always knew about the brutality, but seeing the names and faces of these rapists that were our great-great-great grandfathers was difficult. After several months of grieving, we were able to embrace our entire heritage-African and European. Genealogical research and stories are a great way to celebrate inherited gifts and skills, acknowledge the dysfunction, and start healing a family's lineage.

6. Go On a Parent-Child Date

Take each child out for bonding time (not just for the child's birthday). The date can be anything from a hike to a special dinner out. It communicates value and honor to the child.

7. Self-Care

We can model humility and ownership of personal growth to our kids despite the busyness of life. Practicing a weekly Sabbath, private retreats, and prayer times; getting sufficient sleep, proper nutrition, and exercise; and swapping with another parent for "sitter" time are essential ways to show our kids what practical self-care looks like.

Can We Change Our Friends?

Friendships provide connection, often one that is more satisfying than one's own family relationships. Since we can choose our friendships, changing the culture of a friend group may seem unnecessary because we can find different friends. Friendship is not meant to be one-sided, but allow a mutual exchange. When we're being give something that isn't healthy—opinions, attitudes, or behavior, we need to think about the quality of that friendship. To protect ourselves, we may have to get our relational needs met through more constructive relationships. Though breaking off long-term attachments is emotionally challenging, it is wise to separate from abusive people whose influence undermines our destiny. The Bible teaches that bad companions will corrupt us. When we're comfortable saying no and setting limits, we can embrace our autonomy within any group.

All that being said, if we choose, we can find the patience and ability to maintain a connection with friends who aren't pursuing wholeness. With prayer, the right perspective, and a stable support system, over time, we can help a friend transition from a place of dysfunction to health *if* they choose.

All of us have areas where we need to grow. We don't want to focus on another person's brokenness and not see our own. So we need to stay mindful that each person has their own rate of maturity and self-awareness. Some people simply choose not to change, and although we can choose to stay connected, our expectations of them need to be reasonable.

How Can We Help Change the Course of Our Workplace?

Mutual respect and self-discipline go a long way in any work environment. Culture Changers view every individual as having worth, no matter their unique differences, which means they choose to treat all people with respect. Likewise, seeing every human being as "broken" keeps us from unreasonable expectations and disappointment.

When it comes to influencing our workplace, here is the key: instead of figuring out how to change our workplace culture, we can steer our words, behaviors, and interactions to promote constructive conversations and an exemplary work ethic. This posture takes personal self-discipline—knowing when to speak and when to remain silent, when to engage and when to walk away. We lead the change, but not overtly. We must respect workplace protocol.

Pray for Your Leaders (Pastor, Boss, Teacher, Etc.)

When they're self-aware, the leaders of businesses, organizations, churches, and institutions make a positive impression on their employees or private contractors. Vulnerability in these environments is often counter-intuitive, and countercultural—completely different than what we sense it *should* be to bring foster triune health. If leaders are forthcoming about the areas of weakness they're seeking to strengthen, people will respect them more easily—because people don't like pretense. Additionally, business owners who stress the maintenance of boundaries for home life, work-life, and personal life, and heed these boundaries themselves, will help their employees realize that achieving balance takes desire and discipline.

Identity is an essential factor to consider for both employee and employer. Many people find their value and status through achievement, but wise leaders serve and view their employees as human beings with individual gifts and purposes that are separate from their work duties.

In terms of community support, if you lead an organization or own a business, take time to research the best places to contribute your money or donate goods, and proactively search out people to mentor. Consider providing a paid internship to a teenager and feature the recipient on your website. Or find a person who struggles economically to mentor in the basics of entrepreneurship.

Often those with the best academic records and who come from the best schools are rewarded with opportunities in a vocation. Merit should indeed be rewarded. However, there are many unmotivated young people who—if given a chance—would find the incentive to excel. These are students who get lower grades or perform poorly on tests for various reasons. When employers target these students and offer practical skills, vocational opportunities, and academic incentives, they can help end generational cycles of economic disparity.

Ideally, those of us who have some level of authority—political, financial, corporate, etc.—will come alongside our peers and offer a more constructive lens in which to view life and humanity, and as a consequence, facilitate change where needed.

CHAPTER SIXTEEN

Practical Ideas for Influencing Your Community

It can be challenging to explain to a young inner-city male why so many of his male relatives have been to jail or to retrain teen girls that their character is more important than their outward appearance when the latter is modeled to them on reality TV and in magazines. Similarly, it is no easy task to help a college graduate not become an elitist womanizer like his father and grandfather. In those moments, when we're trying to help someone who is struggling to make better choices, we need to remind ourselves of our past—and present—moments of struggle. Our own bad decisions not only affected us but likely affected our family members and perhaps even our community. From this place of honesty, we can explain with grace, the harm they are doing to the world around them.

We need to keep in mind that people's struggles are often layered with unresolved pain or epigenetic predispositions. What day-to-day challenges continue to trigger negative feelings and behaviors? Perhaps family issues cripple them. When we're helping someone find triune healing, we will likely run into more than just what that person has experienced in their lifetime; we'll also encounter what is written in their DNA and heritage.

Because direct, individual contact is so important, organizations and ministries across the United States are devoted to helping people and transform communities.

In Charlottesville, a few young adult ministry groups have joined arms to serve our residents. This multi-racial, multi-church group of twenty- and thirty-year-olds do projects like grass mowing, painting, and repair. They call themselves, *Catalyst.* Lexi Hutchins, the primary coordinator, shared with me how the traditional way of doing young adult ministry offered more socializing than service, and these young adults wanted more. Serving others is a necessary but often undeveloped part of our humanity—and it carries the power to change lives.

For some, *walking alongside* the hurting is their lifelong assignment. I've had the honor of hearing Amy Lancaster of We Will Go Ministries share what can happen when we walk alongside people who are different than we are, whose lives are a mess, and who believe they have no hope. She and her husband live in an all-black neighborhood in Jackson, Mississippi—an area affected by poverty, crime, and substance abuse, yet they are committed to that land and those people. Her one-on-one engagement with her neighbors has changed lives. The ministry serves and provides training and job opportunities, and some residents have given their lives to Christ. Through determination, commitment, and kindness, a community is slowly being transformed.

Hearing such stories of triumph helps build the faith we need to believe that an individual, a family, and even a community can go from a *destructive* to a *constructive* way of living. Teen moms who benefit from programs like Young Lives talk about the support and confidence they receive from dedicated mentors who volunteer to walk alongside them. Their testimonies reveal not only the challenges of being a single parent but also the practical care and emotional guidance offered by volunteers who want to weep with those who weep and lift up the weary. The care and guidance enable these women to turn around and help others who are going through similar situations. At a 2019 celebration event in Charlottesville, Virginia, one young woman shared how she can now encourage and advise her peers before they experience an unplanned pregnancy. Many of these women who go through the Young Lives program acknowledge a God who rescues and can turn any misstep into a redemptive testimony.

Look Around You

When we extend our horizontal gaze, we see beyond our families, workplaces, and friends to our neighbors, fellow club members, and fellow students. If people perceive you as safe and helpful, they will open up to you. So if you want to influence your neighborhood and outlying communities, be that safe and helpful person.

Serving in Simple Ways

- Ask questions and listen attentively to others. These gestures will strengthen, affirm, and honor them.

- When tragedy happens to someone you know, check-in with that person frequently.

- Don't hide what you believe, but don't teach or give counsel unless asked.

- Offer inspirational videos, podcasts, or articles that may provide further insight to the people you are walking alongside.

- Love your neighbor. Keep an eye on their houses when they're gone. Take them cookies, a Christmas card; invite them to dessert, a potluck cookout, or a game night. You can return their garbage cans from the curb, pick up trash in their yard, trim their bushes, and take meals when someone in the house isn't well. Always greet them when you see them.

- Learn how state and local agencies and governments work so that you can inform individuals who may need financial or debt assistance, substance abuse help, or legal advice.

You will also find organizations and grassroots endeavors that have already navigated through the systemic web to meet needs hands-on. Many of these ground-level operations have figured out how to meet real needs through volunteerism.

Volunteer

Which organizations, churches, or events have been effective to meet people's needs? Find one in which to invest your time and money. Volunteering builds community and puts a face on statistics. Several organizations here in Charlottesville meet a variety of needs, from mentoring to lawn care to providing meals to immobile residents. You'll likely be able to find an organization in your area that does something you enjoy and want to be a part of.

Be Ready for Opportunities

One day I realized that I needed to learn not to be in such a rush when running errands. I needed to allow for extra time—just in case of an unexpected encounter. Begin to think about the people you regularly encounter—the cashier or the bank teller. Do you know their name? You don't need to make awkward introductions and try to insert yourself into someone's life, but be open to those natural opportunities where lives intersect. Be willing to strike up a conversation. As you become more comfortable with the mission of a Culture Changer, you will inevitably meet the right person at the right time. I consider these divine appointments, orchestrated by God.

In addition to these spontaneous meetings, we can reach out in other ways as well—writing a simple note or text to encourage someone we know who is going through a tough season. Is there someone who has recently moved to your area? Transitions can make life difficult, and they would probably welcome a compassionate heart and listening ear. Anticipate people's struggles based on simple facts. Is your child's teacher newly married? Is he fresh out of college? Is she recently divorced?

All these ideas, though simple, are part of being a safe and helpful place for others, a person who helps bring triune healing.

Put the Phone Away

One morning in 2019, I drove to a small coffee shop to write. Two tables away from me was a large white man on his laptop. Only about twenty-four inches away from him in a cushioned chair was a young, slender African American woman on her phone. We were in our worlds but sitting two feet apart. So close, yet worlds apart.

I realized afterward that I needed to be proactive in a world where social etiquette has confined us to invisible walls.

Human interaction has changed over the last several years. Today when we're standing in a line somewhere, most heads will be down looking at smartphone screens. We've become a people who spend so much time on our phones in public that we don't look around at the people standing next to us in line, the other parents supervising their kids at the park, or the fans in the seats around us at a sporting event.

Another day I was working on my laptop in the dining area at a local grocery store. The table was long enough to fit me on one end while another woman was typing on her laptop at the opposite end. I remember wondering if she was a writer too. An hour later, as some of my friends came to join me for fellowship, she rose to leave. As my friends left the table for a moment to get some snacks, I felt a divine nudge to ask the woman if she was a writer. She smiled and said, "Yes." The next several minutes of our conversation was undoubtedly a divine exchange.

She and I exchanged email addresses and met up a few months later for a coffee date. While we shared differing worldviews, we found enough in common to keep the conversation enjoyable. I realized later that the sole purpose for that occasion could be for the people around us to witness a black woman and a white woman meeting together amicably.

The steps of the righteous are ordered by God.[34] Take a risk and start a conversation. Even if it is not a divine encounter, your neighborliness will come against the atmosphere of social distance so prevalent in the U.S. today. We need friendly interaction.

Be reliable. Be faithful. Be encouraging. Be real.

Once rapport is established with people and they've invited you into their situation, don't be afraid to go deep with them. Here are some questions you could ask:

- What is one thing you've accomplished that was meaningful to you?
- What is your favorite memory?
- What do you consider your greatest strength?
- What do you want to change about your life?
- How do you process loss and change?
- How did you deal with [a lousy situation]?
- If you could do anything with your life, what would it be?

These types of questions lead to great conversations that can bring vision and healing.

Testimonies of Healing

A few years ago, a friend introduced me to a young married woman who was dealing with resentment toward her

---

34 Psalm 37:23 The steps of the God-pursuing ones follow firmly in the footsteps of the Lord, and God delights in every step they take to follow him.

mother. When I first heard a general description of the woman's background, my mind automatically categorized her into an economic class and educational status. I also viewed her family in a historical and racial context. But once I met her face to face and heard her heart, those categories dissolved. She was just a young woman going through a tough time.

Her mother had experienced post-partum depression after giving birth to her last child. The young woman, whom I'll call Anne, was a teenager when she was forced to take over her mother's domestic duties and care for her younger siblings. Now, as a young mom of two, she was exhausted. Even though her mother was no longer affected by depression, she stayed emotionally and physically distant and didn't provide any aid.

My friend and I sat down with Anne to discuss the issues she was facing and her family line. As she shared what she knew of the dynamics of her grandparents' life, a pattern of family dysfunction began to reveal itself. Her struggle was much more than class and background, and it could have been anyone's story. We tend to group people together so we can communicate and process quickly—but when we meet a person, we find we need to discard the categories.

Anne's story ends well. We listened, answered her questions, and prayed with her. My friend stayed in close contact with her and, through one-on-one engagement, guided her in how to resolve emotional wounds and inherited patterns of dysfunction. Anne now has the tools to set a new course for her future generations.

Keeping the Whole Person in Mind

To tend to the whole person, Christian counselors and faith-healing practitioners acknowledge that we must enlarge our tool belt to help people be well in all areas of their lives—spirit, soul, and body. Counseling appointments and prayer have the potential to transform a person's inner world, but lifestyle—daily decisions and thought processes—also help personal transformation. Or said another way, diet, exercise, and sleep affect more than our physical bodies! They assist the health of our souls. Certain foods like sugar can have a direct impact on a person's emotional wellbeing, while endorphins released through physical activity relieve mental and emotional stress. Lack of sleep not only leads to psychological distress but can also push a person toward emotional disarray, which affects relationships. How we treat and care for our physical bodies is essential to having good mental and emotional health.

A vast number of alternative therapies for bringing about health and wellbeing are in the process of development as spiritual counselors and health practitioners understand the connection between the physical body and the human soul.

You Will Make A Difference

A good portion of our ability to change communities and impact individuals comes through "living in an opposite spirit" to the divisive and hopeless climate around us, which means that even our *manner* is powerful. Just smiling, saying hi, or asking if someone is having a good day is a great start—and often is enough to affect visible and unseen realities.

When my husband or I, both African Americans, greet and make conversation with Joe, a white policeman who provides security for our church, we're making an impression on his mind about African American people.

When I picked up the umbrella dropped by an older white man on the floor of the grocery store, I planted a seed in his mind that can oppose any discriminatory seed he may have grown up with.

When I've hung out in public with my Asian, Latino, and white friends, heads have turned because it's unusual to see such a grouping in my town. Seeds are planted as you befriend people of other ethnicities and go out to have fun together.

In our faith journey, we can learn how to be led by the Holy Spirit. We know we want to see change—but that desire grows even *stronger* as we remind ourselves it is God's desire, and He's the One who put it in our hearts. Jesus came to heal the broken. His desire is for paths to be made straight and all people to receive peace, wholeness, honor, and dignity. God is undoing what natural and spiritual forces have implemented against humanity. Let's partner with Him.

About the Author

Tina has served as an associate pastor, worship pastor, and prayer ministry director. After homeschooling for twenty years, she began writing while continuing to serve in lay ministry. In 2020 she was certified as an Apprentice Facilitator in Classic Trauma Healing through the American Bible Society. She and her husband have six children and live in Central Virginia. Her other books are Cultivating the Souls of Parents: Facing our Brokenness; Embracing His Likeness. She loves DIY projects and cooking.

www.tinawebb.net
www.instagram.com/tina.w.webb
www.facebook.com/tina.w.webb

I am a Journey Teller,
From desert sands to mountain peaks,
imaginary worlds to life's realities,
I record to remember.
I reflect to discover where the Divine intersects my world.

Recommended Resources

Books

Age of Opportunity by Paul David Tripp

Boundaries by Dr. Henry Cloud and Dr. John Townsend (and other books)

The Case for Christ by Lee Strobel

Created for Influence by William L. Ford

Culture of Honor by Danny Silk

Deep Faith by Rob Reimer

The Happy Intercessor by Beni Johnson

Intentional Parenting by Bill Johnson

Intercessory Prayer by Dutch Sheets

Keep Your Love On by Danny Silk

Mere Christianity by C.S. Lewis

Original Intent by David Barton

The Physics of Heaven by Judy Franklin and Ellyn Davis

Prayer Portions by Sylvia Gunter

Soul Care by Rob Reimer

SOZO by Dawna De Silva and Teresa Liebscher

Switch on Your Brain by Dr. Caroline Leaf

The Soul of Shame by Curt Thompson

Watchman On The Walls by Bruce Anderson, Stephen McDowell, and Mark Beliles

With Christ in the School of Prayer by Andrew Murray

Notable Speakers and Authors
Brene Brown - Researcher, Storyteller

Mike and Lori Cramer, Young Life and Young Lives

Ingrid Davis – Certified Leadership Coach, Speaker

Dr. Joy DeGruy Leary – Researcher, Author

Will Ford - Author

C.S Lewis - Author

Dr. Keith McCurdy – Speaker, President of Total Life Counseling

Stephen McDowell – Author, Speaker; The Providence Foundation

Rev. Dean Nelson - Speaker, Natl Outreach Director for The Human Coalition

Star Parker - Political Activist, Author, President of C.U.R.E

Dr. Rob Reimer - Author, Speaker, Professor at NYACK

Dr. Gayle Rogers - Founder and President of Forever Free, Inc.

Ravi Zacharias - Author, Christian Apologist of RZIM

Websites

https://drleaf.com

ingriddavis.com

https://wewillgo.org/missionaries/david-and-amy-lancaster/

8thmountain.com/about/

Topics to Research Further

Epigenetics and Neuroplasticity

Generational Sin Patterns

Racism and Discrimination

Emotional Maturity and Wellness

Comparative Religion

Intercession

Spiritual Warfare

Conservatism, Liberalism, Progressivism

Effects of Social Media on Families

Relativism and Morality

Quantum Physics